北大版海外汉语教材

CHINA & USA
A Course in Comparison Based on Comparative Culturology

中美国别文化比较教程

II

舒一兵 编著

北京大学出版社
PEKING UNIVERSITY PRESS

图书在版编目（CIP）数据

中美国别文化比较教程 Ⅱ / 舒一兵编著 . —北京：北京大学出版社，2011. 3
(北大版海外汉语教材)
ISBN 978-7-301-18628-2

Ⅰ. 中… Ⅱ . 舒… Ⅲ . 比较文化－中国、美国－对外汉语教学－教材
Ⅳ . ① G04 ② H195.4

中国版本图书馆CIP数据核字（2011）第035377号

书　　名：中美国别文化比较教程 Ⅱ
著作责任者：舒一兵 编著
责 任 编 辑：孙娴 suzannex@126.com
标 准 书 号：ISBN 978-7-301-18628-2/H · 2773
出 版 发 行：北京大学出版社
地　　址：北京市海淀区成府路 205 号 100871
网　　址：http://www.pup.cn
电 子 信 箱：zpup@pup.pku.edu.cn
电　　话：邮购部 62752015　发行部 62750672
出版部 62754962　编辑部 62752028
印 刷 者：北京宏伟双华印刷有限公司
经 销 者：新华书店
787 毫米 ×1092 毫米　16 开本　10.5 印张　194 千字
2011 年 3 月第 1 版　2011 年 3 月第 1 次印刷
印　　数：0001 － 3000 册
定　　价：38.00 元 (附 MP3 盘 1 张)

前 言

选修一门从文化学的角度来解释和比较中国文化和美国文化异同的专题课程，会对更好地掌握中文，了解中国起到十分明显的促进作用，这种作用是其他与中文或中国文化相关的课程取代不了的。作为本书的作者，我真诚希望这个建议能得到认真地考虑。

文化作为一个术语，各个历史时期的学者对它的解释是不同的。19 世纪，英国哲学家、人类学家爱德华·泰勒将文化定义为："所谓文化或文明乃是包括知识、信仰、艺术、道德、法律、习俗以及包括作为社会成员的个人而获得的其他任何能力、习惯在内的一种综合体。"20 世纪以来，人们对于文化概念的阐释日趋精细。美国文化学家克罗伯强调人的行为模式，认为文化包括"行为的模式"和"指导行为的模式"。

20世纪80年代以来，中国有关文化的研究，从各个视角界定文化的概念。学者们的基本共识是：文化从最广泛的意义上说，可以包括人的一切生活方式和为满足这些生活方式所创造的事物，以及基于这些方式所形成的心理和行为。无论对于文化的概念如何阐释，归根结底总离不开人的活动与生活方式。人创造了文化，文化又塑造了人；人推进了文化的生成与发展，文化又影响与造就了人的特性。这种研究文化现象或文化体系的科学就叫做文化学。

比较文化学是对于不同类型文化进行比较研究的学科。所谓不同类型的文化指的是不同的民族、不同的地域、不同的国家所具有的不同文化传统、文化特性、文化发展史与文化形态等。比较文化学是以比较意识、比较思维方式和比较方法为特征的研究学科，而不是简单的形式比较或比附。

文化涉及的对象是人。中国有13亿人。根据人类学家和民族学家的研究，这13亿人中存在着56个民族。其中，汉族的人口最多，因此，其余的民族因人数较少的原因，就被称为"少数民族"，如藏族、维吾尔族、蒙古族、满族等等。虽然他们人数较少，但他们生活的区域却几乎占了中国版图的一半，他们的历史和文化无论在深度上和广度上都影响着中国文化。中国历史上最后的三个朝代，除明朝外，元朝和清朝分别是由蒙古族和满族建立的封建王朝。因此，谈论中国文化时若缺少了少数民族文化，就简直是不可思议的事情。国际著名社会学家、人类学家费孝通博士所提出的中国文化的"多元一体论"，科学而系统地阐述了这一观点。本书的编写也力求以这个理论为首个编写出发点，而不仅仅是围绕着汉族文化。

文化是历史的，也是现代的。有些人理解文化时的一个潜台词就是“历史上、过去的事情”。因此，他们十分注重对传统的研究和介绍，而相比较之下，有些淡化或忽视了对当代的、现实的文化现象的研究。本人认为，当代中国文化，特别是中国改革开放以后的文化，正处于与世界文化相互碰撞、相互融合的一个剧变时期。从未来历史的角度来看，这是最值得研究的一个阶段。我们有幸生活在其中，就更没有理由去忽视其在中国文化研究中的地位了。对现实文化进行比较研究是编写本书的第二个出发点。

在经济全球化的时代，世界上各民族文化的区别界限已呈现出越来越模糊和中和的趋势。我们既要承认“越是民族的，就越是世界的”个性文化，也更应该看到因密切融合而相互渗透的共性文化。文化的对比研究不应只局限在狭义的文学、艺术、民俗等，而是应该放到更广阔的领域去审视，观察比较各国文化因素在教育、经济以及政治上的不同作用。从更宽广的范围着手进行对比研究和现象描述，是编写本书的第三个出发点。

文化是一个民族中全体人民大众创造和拥有的，是由这个民族的文化精英，如这个民族的艺术家、文学家、哲学家、教育家、科学家和宗教圣贤，以及他们的作品和思想所代表的，但民族文化不能简单地等同于精英文化。如果我们的目的是了解和比较这一民族文化的全貌，则更应该去了解这个民族普遍的大众文化，因为精英文化是建立在大众文化的基础上的，没有对大众文化的了解，就谈不上了解精英文化。另外，对精英文化的了解应该是建立在它所属的文化学科基础上的，即只有掌握了对这一文化学科的专业知识，才能够掌握某一精英文化的深邃之处。比如，你只有了解了一个民族普遍的音乐审美取向和大众的演奏、演唱方式，如中国江苏无锡当地的民间小调，才能欣赏音乐大师阿炳的作品，如《二泉映月》的奥妙之处。但这似乎已超出了比较文化学的研究范畴，而属于音乐学这个学科了。与美国不同，中国人口的大多数是农民，中国的农民文化内容丰富，特色鲜明，注重包括农民文化在内的大众文化是编写本书的第四个出发点。

以上四点也表明了本书作者基本的中国文化观。

各位读者需要注意的是，本书不是比较文化学的专著，而是要通过比较文化学的理论和方法去了解中美两国在政治、经济、教育、历史、艺术、民族性格，乃至日常生活方面的异同之处，以提高读者的中文水平，并增进对中国文化及中国人的了解。也正因为这个目的，书中介绍的有关中国文化的信息量要大于有关美国文化的信息量，无论课文还是课后练习，均是如此。作为本书的编者，我猜想学生对美国文化的了解也许多过对中国文化的了解。通过本书，把熟悉的美国文化与仍然陌生的中国文化做一个系统而全面的比较，相信会有助于更容易地了解中国文化。

这套教材共选择了30个文化专题。语法和词汇的安排从易到难。课文中的句型和词汇有很多会与一般中文教科书上的句型和词汇重复，因此选修这门课，也有助于学生中文课的学习。每个课文都附有英文翻译，有些练习和活动也可以用英文完成，这些都会对你有所帮助。

关于本书的具体用法，请参看《使用指南》。

舒一兵

于西雅图

Preface

To select a course which is about commenting and comparing with Chinese culture and American culture will greatly promote understanding Chinese language and culture. This function cannot be replaced by other courses in point of Chinese language and culture. As the author of this book, I honestly hope that my ideas will be considered carefully.

Culture, as a glossary definition, has been commented on differently by scholars in different periods. In the 19th century, British philosopher and anthropologist, Edward Tylor defined the so-called culture or civilization as an integration of knowledge, belief, art, morals, law, convention as well as ability and practice that an individual obtains as a social community member. Since the 20th century, the notion about culture has been explained more precisely. American anthropologist, A.L. Kroeber, explaining the behavior mode of human beings, figures out that culture consists of the behavior mode and the mode of instructing behavior.

Since the 1980's, culture has been defined from different points of view in the related research in China. The consensus of Chinese scholars is that culture, in the most generalized meaning, involves the entire lifestyle of the human being and all the elements of life that aim at satisfying his lifestyle, and mentality and behavior formed from his lifestyle. No matter how one explains the culture, it is impossible to go away from the subject of human activities and lifestyles: humans create culture and culture creates humans; humans advance culture's building and development and culture affects and shapes humans' character. The subject of researching cultural phenomenon and systems is called culturology.

Comparative culturology is the subject of study in comparing various cultural types; the so-called various cultural types refer to the different cultural traditions, characteristics, history and forms of different ethnic groups, regions and countries. Comparative culturology is a subject that relates to characteristics for comparing consciousness, ways of thinking and methodology. It is not a simple formal comparison or analogy.

Culture is about people. There are 1.3 billion people in China. By the research of anthropologists and ethnologists, Chinese people consist of 56 ethnic groups. Thereinto, the population of Chinese Han people is the largest. Due to the smaller population of other ethnic groups, they are named Minorities, such as Tibetan, Uigur, Mongolian and

Manchu. Their living areas cover almost half of China's territory although their population is not the largest. Their history and culture impact Chinese culture either in depth or in extension. The last three dynasties in Chinese history, except Ming, Yuan and Qing are the feudalism dynasties established by Mongolian and Manchu. Therefore, it is unthinkable and unimaginable to discuss Chinese culture without talking about Chinese minorities culture. Dr. Xiaotong Fei, the world famous sociologist and anthropologist, states this view systematically and scientifically by his theory of diversified Chinese cultural factors in one integration. This book is based on and inspired by Dr. Fei's theory and doesn't just address Chinese Han's culture.

Culture is not only historical but modern. Some people understand and study Chinese culture as the things in history and past, so they pay much attention to researching and introducing tradition while neglecting the research in modern and real cultural phenomenon. As the author, I think the modern Chinese culture, especially the Chinese culture after China's reformation and open policy, is in the midst of an upheaval that results in Chinese culture and world culture impacting and compromising one another. In view of the future history, this period is the most worthy of being researched. Fortunately, living in this period, we have no excuse to ignore its status in Chinese culture research. The second intention of this book is to research real and modern culture by comparison.

In the age of economic globalization, the distinguishing finitude of the worldwide national culture presents a trend that becomes more and more ambiguous and neutralized. We should acknowledge either individual culture that is more national, more worldwide, or the common culture that is being penetrated by two or more ethnic groups for close amalgamation. The comparison research in culture should not be only limited in the narrow sense of literature, art, folklore, etc., but should be surveyed in a broader scope to investigate the various functions of how each national cultural factors impact education, economy and politics. To research the comparison and describe phenomenon in a broader scope is the third goal of this book.

The culture is created and possessed by the people of the nation, and is represented by the cultural elite, such as artists, litterateurs, philosophers, educators, scientists and religious oracles, as well as their works and thought. But national culture cannot be equal to national elite culture. If our goal is to understand and compare the overall perspective of the national culture, we should understand the common culture of this nation because elite culture is based on the common culture. Not understanding common culture is not understanding elite culture. On the other hand, to understand a kind of elite culture, one should be prepared to understand the cultural subject which this kind of elite culture belongs to. The core of a kind of elite culture will be understanding nothing other than understanding the special knowledge about the subject. For example, none other than you understand a general musical aesthetic orientation and its popular manner of performance and singing, such as the local chanson in Wuxi, Jiangsu, you will be able to appreciate the music of Master A Bing, for instance, the profundity of his *Two Springs Reflect the Moon (Er Quan Ying Yue)*. But it seems to go beyond the scope of the comparative culturology and belongs to musicology. Differently from the United States, the largest population of China are the peasants; Chinese peasant culture is rich and unique. To pay much attention to popular culture and peasant culture as well is the fourth objective of this book.

The above mentioned four goals of this book also indicate my basic cultural view.

What the readers need to know is this book is not a monograph in comparative culturology; it aims at, by the theory and method of comparative culturology, understanding the difference between the politics, economy, education, history, art, national character, even daily life in China and the United States, to improve readers' ability in Chinese language, and understanding Chinese culture and Chinese people. Just for this target, in the book, the information about Chinese culture is more extensive than the information for the culture of the United States no matter whether in texts and practices behind the texts. As the author, I suspect that the reader's information about American culture may be more than that about Chinese culture. Through this book, comparing the familiar American culture and the unfamiliar Chinese culture systematically and comprehensively will help readers understand Chinese culture more easily.

Thirty cultural topics are focused on in the book. The grammar and words are arranged from the easy to the difficult. Most of the sentence patterns and words in this book are repeated in the textbook of Chinese language art; therefore, this course, will help students in their Chinese language art courses. The English version is attached to each text. Some practices and activities can be done in English; all these will help you.

Regarding how to use this textbook, please refer to *How to Use This Textbook.*

Shu Yibing

Seattle

使用指南

这是一部通过比较文化学的方法，将中国文化学习和汉语习得结合起来，利用短小的课文和大量而形式多样的训练，引导汉语学习者了解中国文化，并掌握一定汉语技能的教科书，是对主干汉语教材的一个有益补充。

一、本书简介

1. 课文字数与内容

本教材分上下两册，共30课。课文分中国和美国两个部分。从第一课到第十课，课文约有汉字500个左右；从第十一课到第二十课，课文约有汉字600个左右；从第二十一课到第三十课，课文约有汉字700个左右。

三十个课文在内容上可分为六个单元。每个单元的大致内容如下：

第一单元：从第一课到第五课，主要介绍和比较中美两国的国家概况；

第二单元：从第六课到第十课，主要介绍和对比两国人民的日常生活；

第三单元：从第十一课到第十五课，主要介绍和对比中美两国人民的休闲娱乐；

第四单元：从第十六课到第二十课，主要介绍和比较两国的教育；

第五单元：从第二十一课到第二十五课，主要介绍和比较两国的政治和社会差异；

第六单元：从第二十六课到第三十课，主要介绍和比较两国的经济、文化及民族性格。

2. 词汇和专有名词

词汇包括课文中的基本生词和短语。专有名词单列。

3. 练习

练习有判断、选择、问答以及资料搜集、探索、讨论和报告七个内容。前三项内容主要是考查对课文的阅读理解情况；而后四项内容的主要目的是引导、帮助读者扩展某一专题下的有关中国文化的知识量，并对某一中国文化专题进行分析、讨论和演讲，以增强对问题的理解和研究的兴趣。有些活动的设计是学生之间，或师生之间互动性的，需要学生集体完成，或通过教师的指导和参与完成。

4. 信息链接

信息链接的主要功能是帮助读者更好地理解课文，顺利完成练习，并增加关于中国文化的知识量。所推荐的网站中，有些是中文的，如果你阅读时有困难，可以借助汉英词典。这里建议读者使用翻译软件“金山词霸http://www.iciba.com/”里的屏幕取词功能，它十分快捷方便，并且可免费使用。其他的翻译软件也可使用，如：

http://cidian.youdao.com/

http://www.tigernt.com/cedict.shtml

http://www.mandarintools.com/worddict.html

http://dictionary.reverso.net/english-chinese/

http://www.lexiconer.com/ceresult.php

5. 英语译文

每课的最后部分是课文的英语译文，它能帮助学生正确理解汉语课文的意思。

汉语水平尚未提高的学生也可以在读完英语译文后，用英语做一些有关中国文化方面的练习和活动，这样依然有助于读者理解中国文化，并提高学习汉语的兴趣和能力。

6. 答案

针对每课练习中的“判断”和“选择”两题，给出参考答案。

二、使用方法

1. 作为学生，如何确定本教材是否合适?

（1）阅读课文目录及部分课文的英语译文，看看其大部分内容是不是平时感兴趣的文化专题，并考虑你是否具备关于这些专题所涉及的美国文化方面的知识。

（2）翻阅每课的词汇表，与目前学习的汉语教材的词汇表相比较，看看重合率是否在40%以上。

（3）作为汉语初学者，请看看是否对课文内容、练习感兴趣。请注意：你的中文水平并不是选修本课程的障碍，因为，本课程以了解中国文化为主要目的，学习中文为次要目的，是从比较文化学的角度辅助学生学习中文的。

（4）向教师咨询。

（5）试听一周的课，然后再做决定。

2. 建议的教学安排

（1）课时安排：每课一般用3～5课时完成。建议的课时安排是，课文部分需1～2课时，练习和活动部分需2～3课时。

（2）要求学生预习。

（3）作为课后作业，要求学生完成大部分练习及活动项目。

（4）每课至少安排一次报告或讨论。

3. 如何处理课文与练习之间的关系

可以发现，在一课中，课文比较短小简单，而练习量却比较大。这是因为，作者认为即使课文文字再长，内容再丰富，也难以把一个文化现象讲得全面周到，还反而会影响学生对中国文化的知识扩展和独立研究，并难以从中美两国的文化比较中得出自己的结论。因此，课文只是一个简单的“开场白”，或“启发点”，起引导作用。

另有一点需要着重说明，练习中关于中国文化的成分大于关于美国文化的成分，这是因为本书编写目的是为需要学习中文和了解中国文化的学生服务的，从情理上来讲，这些学生对美国文化的了解应该远远多于对中国文化的了解。

除“判断”、“选择”和“问答”之外，其余的练习用中文或英文完成均可。

4. 如需进一步了解或讨论本书使用方法，请函至本书作者：

edmondshu@yahoo.com

How to Use This Textbook

This is a textbook that integrates learning about Chinese culture and acquiring Chinese language skills by the method of comparative culturology. As a salutary supplement for the Chinese language art textbook the reader is using, it applies short and easy-reading texts as well as mass and multiform exercises to induce Chinese language beginners to understand Chinese culture and learn Chinese language.

1. Introduction

A. Chinese character count and content of the text

This two-volume book consists of 30 lessons. There are two parts addressing China and the USA in each text. There are about 500 Chinese characters in each text from Lesson 1 to Lesson 10, about 600 Chinese characters in each text from Lesson 11 to Lesson 20, and about 700 Chinese characters in each text from Lesson 21 to Lesson 30.

By the contents, the thirty texts can be divided into 6 units; the overall content of each unit is the following:

The first unit, from Lesson 1 to Lesson 5, covers the overview of China and the USA;

The second unit, from Lesson 6 to Lesson 10, covers the lifestyle of both peoples;

The third unit, from Lesson 11 to Lesson 15, covers entertainment;

The fourth unit, from Lesson 16 to Lesson 20, covers education;

The fifth unit, from Lesson 21 to Lesson 25, covers the social and political differences;

The sixth unit, from Lesson 26 to Lesson 30, covers the economy, culture and national character.

B. Words and phrases

Words include the basic words and phrases in the text. The proper nouns are listed separately.

C. Practice

The practice consists of True-False Questions, Multiple Choice, Short Answer Questions and Data Collection, Exploration, Discussion as well as Presentation. The first three practice aim at evaluating reader's reading comprehension, and the final four practice aim at directing and helping readers to know more about Chinese culture regarding to a certain topic, and then do some research, discussion and presentation about it. It will improve the understanding of the topic and increasing the interest in it. Some pracitce must be performed in an interaction of students, or, between teacher(s) and students. They are required to be completed by a group or through the instruction and participation of teacher(s).

D. Information link

The key function of the information link is to help readers understand texts better, complete the practice successfully, and expand knowledge of Chinese culture. Some of the recommended web-sites are in Chinese. If you find it difficult to read, you can look up new words in a Chinese-English dictionary. The function of the open cursor translator of www.iciba.com is recommended because it is fast and free. The other translator softwares can be used as well, such as:

http://cidian.youdao.com/

http://www.tigernt.com/cedict.shtml

http://www.mandarintools.com/worddict.html

http://dictionary.reverso.net/english-chinese/

http://www.lexiconer.com/ceresult.php

E. English version of the text

The last part of each lesson is an English Version of the Text; it is helpful to understand the Chinese text precisely. The readers who are in lower level of Chinese language proficiency can do some practice and activities about Chinese culture after reading the English version, and increase their interest and ability in learning the language.

F. Keys to exercises

The keys to True-False Questions and Multiple Choice of each lesson are given for reference.

2. How to use this textbook

A. As a student, how to know this textbook is a right selection for you?

a. Read the text catalog and some English version to see if most of the contents are the cultural topics you are interested in and if you have background information about the relevant American culture.

b. Skim the Vocabulary behind each text and compare it with your textbook to see if the superposition is above 40%.

c. If you are just a Chinese language beginner, please see if you are interested in the text and practice. Please notice that your Chinese language level is not a barrier to select this course, because the main target of this book is to understand Chinese culture, and the sub-target is to learn Chinese language. It assists students in learning Chinese by comparative culturology.

d. Talk about it with your teacher.

e. Decide after a 1-week trial.

B. The suggested teaching arrangement

a. Hour: each lesson can be completed in 3-5 hours. The suggested breakup of hours is 1-2 hour(s) for text, 2-3 hours for practice and activities.

b. Students are required to make a preparation.

c. As the homework, students are required to complete the majority of practice and activities.

d. A presentation or a discussion for each lesson should be held at least once each week.

3. How to manage the text, practice and activity

It can be seen that each text is short and the practice is long. This is because the author thinks even if the text would be longer, and its content would be richer, it is hard to explain a cultural phenomenon roundly and entirely, and on the contrary, it will even interfere with students' knowledge extension and independent research on Chinese culture and they would have difficulty reaching conclusions of their own by comparing cultures between China and the USA. Therefore, the text is only a prologue or an inspiration, playing a role of guide.

Another point which needs to be stressed is that the component about Chinese culture in practice is longer than the one about American culture because the book is for the students who need to learn Chinese language art and understand Chinese culture. If you are not at the precondition, you have to spend more time learning American culture.

Except for the True-False Questions, Multiple Choice and Short Answer Questions in practice, the rest can be completed in Chinese or English.

4. If you need more information or discussion on how to use this book, please contact the author via edmondshu@yahoo.com.

目录 CONTENTS

第十六课 校服和牛仔裤 1
Lesson 16 School Uniforms and Jeans

第十七课 我的课堂 10
Lesson 17 My Class

第十八课 男生和女生 19
Lesson 18 Boys and Girls

第十九课 作业和考试 27
Lesson 19 Homework and Tests

第二十课 我的学校 35
Lesson 20 My School

第二十一课 街道办事处和社区委员会 44
Lesson 21 Subdistrict Administration and Community Committee

第二十二课 农民 54
Lesson 22 Peasant

第二十三课 选举 64
Lesson 23 Elections

第二十四课 共和与联邦 74
Lesson 24 Republic and Federation

第二十五课 战争与和平 84
Lesson 25 War and Peace

第二十六课 中国制造和美国制造 94
Lesson 26 Made in China and Made in USA

第二十七课　袜子和飞机 105
Lesson 27　Socks and Airplanes

第二十八课　京剧和好莱坞 116
Lesson 28　Beijing Opera and Hollywood

第二十九课　相声和脱口秀 126
Lesson 29　Cross Talk and Talk Show

第 三 十 课　我爱你 135
Lesson 30　I Love You

部分练习答案 144
Keys to Exercises

词汇总表 147
Vocabulary

Xiàofú hé niúzǎikù
第十六课 校服和牛仔裤
Lesson 16 School Uniforms and Jeans

中国的很多中小学都要求学生在学校里穿校服，因为学校认为校服有以下几个好处：一、穿上校服，在校园里就很容易辨认出谁是学生，谁不是学生，便于学校的管理；二、避免有的学生穿破衣服，而被其他同学嘲笑；三、很少有学校有校车接送学生，所以司机们很容易注意到穿着校服走在路上的学生，从而保证孩子们的安全；四、大多数学校没有学生衣柜，校服基本都是运动服的款式，所以学生穿校服便于上体育课。

学生在家的时候，他们有的人喜欢穿牛仔裤和T恤衫，有的人则喜欢穿李宁牌的运动衣。“耐克”、

"阿迪达斯"、"彪马"在中国年青人中也很流行。当然,也有的学生认为穿什么都无所谓。穿校服好不好,一直是老师、学生和家长讨论的问题。

美国的大多数中小学不要求学生穿校服，有的教会学校和私立学校可能会要求穿。很多人认为穿校服影响了个人穿衣的爱好和自由。如果都穿校服的话，也显得单调和呆板。在美国，学生的家离学校都比较远，走路或骑车上学都需要很长时间，所以几乎所有的学校都为学生提供校车。学校里有学生衣柜和更衣室，有体育课时，学生可以先把运动衣放在衣柜里，上课前再去更衣室换上；也有的学生为了方便，直接在里面穿上运动衣，然后再穿上牛仔服等外衣。

总的来讲，美国学生在学校里的穿着选择是自由的，运动衣一般只在运动的时候才穿。大部分学生平常就穿牛仔裤、T 恤衫和夹克衫等。这一点和中国学生不太一样。

词汇 Vocabulary

校服 xiàofú	school uniform
牛仔裤 niúzǎikù	jeans
穿 chuān	wear, put on
好处 hǎochù	advantage, benefit, good
校园 xiàoyuán	campus
辨认 biànrèn	distinguish, identify
嘲笑 cháoxiào	laugh at, deride
校车 xiàochē	school bus
衣柜 yīguì	locker
便于 biànyú	convenient for
体育课 tǐyùkè	physical education
运动服 yùndòngfú	sportswear

款式 kuǎnshì	design, pattern, style
穿着 chuānzhuó	dressing, wearing
T恤衫 T xùshān	T-shirt
流行 liúxíng	popular
教会 jiàohuì	church
私立 sīlì	private
显得 xiǎnde	look, seem
呆板 dāibǎn	stiffness
提供 tígōng	provide, offer
更衣室 gēngyīshì	changing room
外衣 wàiyī	outerwear
夹克衫 jiākèshān	jacket

专有名词 Proper Nouns

李宁 Lǐ Níng	LI-NING
耐克 Nàikè	Nike

阿迪达斯 Ādídásī	Adidas
彪马 Biāomǎ	Puma

课文理解
Understanding of the Text

一、判 断 True-false questions

1. 穿上校服，在校园里就很容易辨认谁是学生，谁不是学生。 ☐ 对 ☐ 错
2. 有的学生穿破衣服，会被其他同学嘲笑。 ☐ 对 ☐ 错
3. 很多校服都不采用运动服的款式。 ☐ 对 ☐ 错
4. 中国学生在家也必须穿校服。 ☐ 对 ☐ 错
5. 美国学生和中国学生一样，都要穿校服。 ☐ 对 ☐ 错

二、选 择 Multiple choice

1. 中国很多学校要求学生穿______。
   A. 阿迪达斯　B. 李宁运动服　C. 彪马　D. 校服
2. 中国学生穿校服是为了______。
   A. 老师看不见　B. 便于管理　C. 保证安全　D. 有衣柜
3. 中国学校接送学生的校车很______。
   A. 少　B. 小　C. 大　D. 多
4. 美国学生的家一般离学校都比较______，所以很多学生都______去学校。
   A. 近　B. 远　C. 走路　D. 坐校车　E. 骑车
5. 课文中说，美国学生在学校的穿着是______。
   A. 被限制的　B. 自由的　C. 漂亮的　D. 难看的

三、问 答 Short answer questions

查阅一下李宁牌服装的历史。

Please look up the history of LI-NING Brand.

信息链接
Information Link

http://www.china.com.cn/ch-shaoshu/index.htm
http://www.efu.com.cn/
http://www.li-ning.com.cn/
http://www.paulnoll.com/China/Minorities/
http://www.marlamallett.com/
http://www.chinatownconnection.com/
http://www.mysteriouschina.com/
http://www.stylishcn.com/
http://chineseculture.about.com/
http://www.schoolbusfleet.com/
http://www.schoolbusinfo.org/
http://www.chinasmack.com/
http://www.xdxx.com.cn/
http://hi.baidu.com/cctvbus555

资料搜集
Data Collection

雅戈尔 YOUNGOR

汉语拼音______________________________

以纯服饰 Yishion

汉语拼音____

波司登 Bosideng

汉语拼音____

报喜鸟 Saint Angel

汉语拼音____

美特斯·邦威 Meters Bonwe

汉语拼音____

拓展活动
Extention

一、探索 Exploration

请查阅下面是中国哪些民族的服装:
Please look up which Chinese nationality the costume belongs to:

_______族 Nationality

_______族 Nationality

_______族 Nationality

_______族 Nationality

_______族 Nationality

_______族 Nationality

二、讨论 Discussion

1. 传统文化对中国校服有影响吗?
   Does the traditional Chinese culture influence Chinese school uniforms?
2. 李宁公司为什么要用"*Make the Change*"这句话作为广告词?
   Why is *Make the Change* the advertisement message of LI-NING Company?

三、报告 Presentation

从中国人的服装变化看中国社会的演变。

Observing the changes in Chinese society by observing the changes of Chinese costume.

英语译文
English Version of the Text

Most Chinese elementary schools and high schools require students to wear uniforms, because the schools think there are several advantages to it. First, it is easy to identify who a student is or not. Second, it can prevent the student wearing torn and used clothing from being laughed at. Third, drivers can easily take notice of a walking student who wears a school uniform and guarantee their safety because most schools do not have school buses. And fourth, wearing school uniforms is convenient for students to take physical education courses because most schools have no lockers for students, and many school uniforms are in the style of sportswear.

At home, some students like wearing jeans and T-shirts, some prefer sportswear such as the brand LI-NING. Nike, Adidas and Puma are also popular among young people in China. Of course, some students don't care what they are wearing at all. Teachers, students and parents have talked about the topic, "Is it good or bad for students to wear school uniforms?" for a long time.

Most American elementary schools and high schools don't require student to wear uniforms, while some Christian schools and private schools do. Many people think that wearing school uniforms affects personal dressing individuality and freedom. If students are required to wear school uniforms, they will look blank and stiff. In the United States, the schools are far away from students' homes; students have to take lots of time to walk or ride bicycles to school, so most schools provide school buses. There are lockers and changing rooms for students; they can put their sportswear in them and change it if they have physical education class. Some students wear the sportswear underneath for their convenience, and then wear outerwear, such as jeans on top of their sportswear.

Generally speaking, American students are free to wear their favorite clothing in school, and sportswear is only used when doing sports. Most students just wear jeans, T-shirts and jackets most of the time. This is a little different from Chinese students.

17 第十七课 我的课堂

Wǒ de kètáng

Lesson 17 My Class

在中国，一般来讲，课堂上，学生们安静地坐着听老师上课，即使有听不懂的地方，也很少在课堂上马上问老师，而是要等到下课以后再问。这是为什么呢？可能有以下几个原因：一、学生不愿意打断老师的正常授课；二、认为问题可能只是自己的，别的同学已经明白了；三、认为自己的问题可能太简单、太"愚蠢"，问出来会被大家笑话；四、担心老师埋怨自己因个人问题耽误了课堂教学。正因为这些方方面面的考虑，在中国的课堂上，学生们就显得特别安静。

当然，上面说的都是一些表面原因。要从根本上去分析的话，这与中国的儒家文化和中国人的性格有很大关系。

向孔子像行礼

中国的一堂教学示范课

在美国，一般来讲，学生在课堂上一旦有问题，可以随时问老师，老师也乐于回答学生们各种各样的问题。这样，从一个问题开始，一节课就很有可能变成了老师和学生们共同参加的讨论课，使学生从讨论中获得知识或思路。很多老师还把学生在课堂上提问和发表意见的表现，计算成分数，写在学生的成绩单里。因此，与中国的课堂相比，美国的课堂是活跃而热闹的。这反映出了与中国传统儒家文化不同的教育观。在儒家文化里，虽然也承认教学和学习的相互促进作用，但更强调的是尊重教师的威严，及对其所教授知识的“无条件”服从。这种观点，与西方的教育观有很大的不同。

中西方的教育观对比研究，是一项十分有意义的工作。

词 汇 Vocabulary

打断 dǎduàn	interrupt, break in
授课 shòu kè	teach
愚蠢 yúchǔn	stupid
埋怨 mányuàn	complain, blame
耽误 dānwù	delay, hold up
表面 biǎomiàn	surface, exterior
根本 gēnběn	essential, substance
分析 fēnxī	analysis
儒家 rújiā	confucian
一旦 yídàn	once
乐于 lèyú	be willing to, take pleasure in
变成 biànchéng	become, turn into
获得 huòdé	achieve, obtain

思路 sīlù	reasoning, train of thought
计算 jìsuàn	calculate
分数 fēnshù	mark, point, score
成绩单 chéngjìdān	transcript
承认 chéngrèn	admit, accept
促进 cùjìn	improve
作用 zuòyòng	action, function
强调 qiángdiào	emphasis, stress
尊重 zūnzhòng	defer to, respect
威严 wēiyán	dignity, reverence
无条件 wú tiáojiàn	unconditional
服从 fúcóng	obedience, submit

课文理解
Understanding of the Text

一、判 断 True-false questions

1. 中国学生一般不愿意打断老师的正常授课。 □对 □错
2. 中国学生担心他的问题只是自己的，别的同学已经明白了，因此不愿意马上向老师提问。 □对 □错
3. 中国学生在课堂上遇到问题，就特别喜欢马上向老师提问。 □对 □错
4. 中国的教育观受儒家思想的影响很大。 □对 □错
5. 美国和中国的教育观十分相似。 □对 □错

二、选 择 Multiple choice

1. 中国学生在课堂上有问题很少马上提问的原因是______。
   A. 学生认为自己的问题太简单，怕别人笑话
   B. 担心影响老师授课
   C. 老师回答问题要收费
   D. 认为别的同学已经明白了
2. ______受儒家思想的影响比较大。
   A. 英国学生 B. 中国学生 C. 美国学生 D. 德国学生
3. 美国学生______在课堂上问老师问题。
   A. 经常 B. 不经常
4. 美国老师会把学生在课堂上提问和发表意见的表现，计算成______，写在学生的成绩单里。
   A. 钱 B. 分数
5. 与中国的课堂相比，美国的课堂比较______。
   A. 活跃 B. 安静

三、问 答 Short answer questions

1. 课文里提出关于中国学校的课堂上比较安静的原因有哪四点？
   What are the four points that explain why Chinese classroom is comparatively quiet in the text?

2. 美国学生和中国学生的课堂表现有何区别?
What kind of differences are there in the classroom between USA and China?

信息链接 Information Link

http://www.artx.cn/artx/jiaoyu/list_4_1.html
http://www.chinakongzi.org/
http://www.zhuangzi.com/zzzb/index.asp
http://www.thetao.info/tao/simplified.htm
http://www.chinamozi.com/
http://www.guoxue.com/master/caiyuanpei/caiyuanpei.htm
http://www.taoxingzhi.org/
http://www.kzxy.com.cn/
http://www.hanban.edu.cn/
http://www.eol.cn/
http://www.cbe21.com/
http://www.asianinfo.org/asianinfo/china/pro-education.htm
http://www.index-china.com/index-english/education-s.htm
http://www.csupomona.edu/~plin/ls201/confucian2.html
http://www.quotationspage.com/quotes/
http://www.confucius.org/
http://taoism.about.com/od/laotzu/qt/Laozi.htm
http://www.daoisopen.com/ZhuangziTranslation.html
http://www.shaoxing.gov.cn/en/0307/10337.htm
http://www.johndeweyef.org/content/view/19/lang,EN
http://www.edu.cn/english_1369/index.shtml
http://www.answers.com/topic/tao-xingzhi
http://www.txzmuseum.org.cn/

资料搜集
Data Collection

孔子 Confucius

汉语拼音________________________________

老子 Laozi

汉语拼音________________________________

庄子 Zhuangzi

汉语拼音________________________________

墨子 Mozi

汉语拼音________________________________

孟子 Mencius

汉语拼音______________________________

蔡元培 Dr. Cai Yuanpei

汉语拼音______________________________

胡适 Dr. Hu Shi

汉语拼音______________________________

陶行知 Dr. Tao Xingzhi

汉语拼音______________________________

拓展活动
Extention

一、探索 Exploration

谈谈你身边的中国同学给你的印象。

Talk about your impression of Chinese students around you.

二、讨论 Discussion

如果你的学校有孔子学院或孔子学堂，你会选修它们的课程吗？

If there is a Confucius Institute or a Confucius Class, do you want to select its courses?

三、报告 Presentation

儒家思想对中国教育的影响。

The influence of Confucianism on Chinese education.

英语译文
English Version of the Text

In the Chinese classroom, generally speaking, students are seated quietly and listen to their teacher. Even if a student cannot understand very well, he seldom asks his teacher a question right away. Why? There are several reasons. First, the student is not willing to interrupt the teacher. Second, he thinks that this question is probably only his own; other classmates don't have it. Third, he thinks that his question is too simple and stupid; he will be laughed at if he asks. Fourth, he worries that the teacher will blame him for holding the class up. Because of these considerations, students look very quiet in the Chinese classroom.

Obviously, the above mentioned are the reasons on the surface. If explaining its true nature in depth, it relates much to Chinese Confucianism and Chinese character.

In a class in the United States, generally speaking, once a student has a question, he can ask the teacher at any time. In this way, a class could become a discussion that all the students join from the student's question, and students will achieve the knowledge or reasoning from the discussion. Lots of teacher mark the student's activities of consultation and presentation, and document it in student's transcripts. Therefore, compared to the classes in China, American classes are more lively and busy. This reflects a different educational viewpoint from Chinese Confucianism. In Confucianism, the interaction between teaching and learning is acknowledged, but the respect for the stateliness of the teacher and the acceptance of the knowledge of the teacher unconditionally is more stressed. This is quite different from the Western educational viewpoint.

Comparative research in educational viewpoints between China and the United States is a very meaningful work.

第十八课 男生和女生

Nánshēng hé nǚshēng

Lesson 18 Boys and Girls

性心理学家认为，一般来讲，当男生和女生到了中学时期，性别意识就有所加强，从相互排斥，发展到了相互吸引的阶段，“校园恋爱”就成了一个普遍现象。为了让学生把精力更多地集中在学习上，中国的老师和家长就尽量避免和阻止学生们过早恋爱，因此还产生了学生和老师、家长之间的矛盾。

有的学者认为，最近这些年中国校园恋爱的情况越来越严重的原因之一，与在中国的传统文化里，一直在性的问题上，对青少年采取回避的态度有关。因为，越是回避，学生们就越是好奇，校园恋爱的现象就越多。目前在中国的不少学校都开设了“性知识”这门课。但似乎事与愿违，校园恋爱现象并没有因开设“性知识”这门课而减少。

美国的校园恋爱情况也很多。不仅如此，未成年人怀孕是否可以堕胎，也已经成为教师、家长、社会工作者、宗教人士，甚至政治家们经常探讨、争论的一个话题。巴拉克·奥巴马总统曾在一所大学演讲时说："也许我们不同意堕胎，但我们仍然认为妇女这些令人心痛的决定并不是随意地做出的"，他说，"让我们一同努力去减少堕胎妇女的数量，减少意外怀孕……并为这些试图生产的妇女提供关注和支持。"①

中国的"学生妈妈"也许没有美国那么多，可能与中国的堕胎合法化有关。但堕胎不仅是一个重要的校园问题，也已经成为了一个严肃的社会问题。无论中国还是美国的男生女生都应该认真考虑。

① 巴拉克·奥巴马总统2009年5月在美国一所天主教大学的演讲。

词汇
Vocabulary

心理学家 xīnlǐ xuéjiā	psychologist
意识 yìshi	consciousness
加强 jiāqiáng	enhance, reinforce
排斥 páichì	exclude, fight off
吸引 xīyǐn	allure, attract
恋爱 liàn'ài	love, amativeness
精力 jīnglì	energy, vigor
集中 jízhōng	concentrate
尽量 jǐnliàng	do one's best
阻止 zǔzhǐ	prevent, stop
过早 guò zǎo	early, premature
矛盾 máodùn	contradiction, conflict

回避 huíbì	avoid
好奇 hàoqí	be curious
事与愿违 shì yǔ yuàn wéi	not go according to plan
怀孕 huái yùn	pregnancy, be pregnant
堕胎 duò tāi	abort, abortion
宗教 zōngjiào	religion
探讨 tàntǎo	discuss
争论 zhēnglùn	argue, dispute
努力 nǔlì	effort, strive, struggle
意外 yìwài	unintended
试图 shìtú	attempt to, try
合法化 héfǎhuà	legalize; legalization

课文理解
Understanding of the Text

一、判 断 True-false questions

1. 性心理学家认为，校园恋爱是正常的现象。 □ 对 □ 错
2. 中国的老师和家长支持学生谈恋爱。 □ 对 □ 错
3. 在中国传统文化里，对性采取回避的态度。 □ 对 □ 错
4. 美国人不关心堕胎的问题。 □ 对 □ 错
5. 在中国，堕胎是合法的。 □ 对 □ 错

二、选 择 Multiple choice

1. 性心理学家认为，学生到了中学时代，性别意识就有所加强，从互相______到互相______。
   A. 排斥　　B. 吸引
2. 在中学阶段，“______”成了一个普遍现象。
   A. 校车　　B. 校园恋爱
3. 在中国传统文化里，在性的问题上，一直对青少年采取______的态度。
   A. 回避　　B.不回避
4. 在______，堕胎是大家争论的一个话题。
   A. 中国　　B. 美国
5. “校园恋爱”和“堕胎”已经成为中国和美国重要的______问题。
   A. 经济　　B. 交通　　C. 宗教　　D. 社会

三、问 答 Short answer questions

1. 中国开设性知识课程的效果怎么样？
   What is the effect of the course of gender knowledge in China?
2. 在美国都有哪些人士关心堕胎问题？
   Who cares about abortion in the United States?

信息链接
Information Link

http://www.china.com.cn/ch-jieri/qixi/1.htm
http://www.hongshuihe.org/viewthread.php?tid=416
http://www.holidays5.com/view/5567.html
http://www.xjtour.net/
http://www.zgxywhxh.com/
http://www.xiaoyuanlife.com/
http://features.cultural-china.com/adultceremony/index.html
http://www.chcp.org/wedding.html
http://www.worldweddingtraditions.com/
http://www.warriortours.com/intro/marriage.htm
http://traditions.cultural-china.com/
http://www.study-in-china.org/LivingInChina/CampusLife/
http://www.religioustolerance.org/abortion.htm
http://www.friesian.com/
http://www.abortiontv.com/
http://www.chinapictures.org/

资料搜集
Data Collection

七夕节 Chinese Valentine's Day

汉语拼音＿＿＿＿＿＿＿＿＿＿＿＿＿＿＿＿＿＿＿＿

抛绣球 Throwing the Rolled Colored Silk Ball

汉语拼音____________________

歌墟节 Singing Festival

汉语拼音____________________

姑娘追 Game of Gu Niang Zhui (Being chased by a girl)

汉语拼音____________________

闹洞房 Teasing the Bride and Bridegroom

汉语拼音____________________

拓展活动
Extention

一、探索 Exploration

谈一谈下面的内容：

Please talk about the following contents:

1. "校园恋爱"和"校园暴力"的成因。

   The reasons for campus dating and the reasons for campus violence.

2. 儒家学说中的男女关系和夫妻关系。

   The relationship between male and female, husband and wife in Confunianism.

二、讨论 Discussion

堕胎在中国合法吗？在美国呢？为什么？

Is the abortion legal in China? Is it legal in the United States? Why?

三、报告 Presentation

中美两国成人礼的比较。

The comparison of coming-of-age ceremonies in China and the United States.

英语译文
English Version of the Text

Most sexual psychologists state that, generally speaking, when boys and girls are at the age of going to high school, their gender consciousness will have been enhanced; they go into the period from being mutually exclusive to being attracted to each other, so campus dating is popular. In order to make sure that students focus on their studies, Chinese teachers and parents do their best to prevent students from experiencing early dating; consequently, conflict between students and teachers as well as parents happens.

Some scholars think that one of the reasons why campus dating has become more and more serious in recent years in China is that it relates to constant discouragement of young men talking about sex by Chinese traditional culture. Because of more discouragement there is more curiosity, and campus dating happens more. Therefore, at the present, many Chinese schools have set up a course of gender knowledge. However, things go contrary to one's wishes, campus dating has not been reduced as a result of this course.

There is much campus dating in the United States. In addition, legal abortion of teenagers has been a popular topic that teachers, parents, social workers, religious believers, even politicians discuss and argue about often. The president Barack Obama said when he gave a lecture, "Maybe we won't agree on abortion, but we can still agree that this heart-wrenching decision for any woman is not made casually..." He went on to say, "So let us work together to reduce the number of women seeking abortions, let's reduce unintended pregnancies... Let's provide care and support for women who do carry their children to term."

The number of "mom-student" in China are much fewer than in the United States; this probably has something to do with abortion legalization. Abortion is not only a very important problem of school culture, but a serious social issue. Both the students in China and in the United States will have to think about it carefully.

第十九课 作业和考试

Zuòyè hé kǎoshì

Lesson 19 Homework and Tests

作业和考试是学生们经常碰到的两个事情，但教育制度不同，作业和考试的内容也就有所不同了。从实质上讲，中国的教育主要是"应试教育"，即教师的一切教学活动和学生的一切学习活动基本上都是围绕着"考试"来进行的。因此，在中国的学校，老师留的作业往往就是所教内容的习题，难易程度可能不同，但不会有太多的讨论性题目，也不会安排太多的课外读物让学生去充实课本以外的知识。

高考发榜

一所中国大学的新生报到现场

考试，特别是初中升高中和高中升大学的考试，是中国学生所面临的最重要的考试，考试成绩甚至会影响学生的一生。中国的高考被称为世界上学术水平最高的大学入学考试。应试教育制度下，中国学生的知识结构和美国学生相比，存在着很大的不同。

美国的教育主要属于“素质教育”，与“应试教育”不同，它更关心学生知识结构的全面性和对问题的分析、探索能力。老师给学生留的作业也基本上是讨论性的习题和大量的课外读物。考试成绩也不一定完全以学生的试卷成绩为主，老师也会考虑学生平时的课堂表现和测验。另一个与中国不同的是，美国没有全国统一的大学入学考试，每个学校会根据自己的标准来录取学生。

采取什么样的教育制度，与一个国家的传统文化有关，也与学生和学校的数量有关。在过去，中国的教学资源相对匮乏，应试教育制度可能比较符合国家的实际情况。但这些年，在中国，素质教育更被重视，考试制度也有了很大的变化。

美国学生在考试

词汇 Vocabulary

教育 jiàoyù	education
内容 nèiróng	content
应试教育 yìngshì jiàoyù	examination-oriented education
围绕 wéirào	enclose, surround
进行 jìnxíng	carry through, process
习题 xítí	exercise subject
程度 chéngdù	degree, grade
题目 tímù	subject
面临 miànlín	be confronted with, face
成绩 chéngjì	achievement, grades
高考 gāokǎo	national matriculation examination

素质教育 sùzhì jiàoyù	quality-oriented education
全面 quánmiàn	full range, comprehensive
能力 nénglì	ability
测验 cèyàn	test
标准 biāozhǔn	standard
资源 zīyuán	resource
匮乏 kuìfá	lack
符合 fúhé	accord with, fit
实际 shíjì	actuality
重视 zhòngshì	pay attention to

课文理解 Understanding of the Text

一、判断 True-false questions

1. 中国目前采取的主要是“素质教育”，美国采取的主要是“应试教育”。 □ 对 □ 错

2. 中国的老师经常要求学生读课外书。 □对 □错
3. 小学的入学考试是中国学生最重要的考试。 □对 □错
4. 中国的高考是世界上学术水平最高的大学入学考试。 □对 □错
5. 采取什么样的教育制度，与一个国家的传统文化有关，也与学生和学校的数量有关。 □对 □错

二、选 择 Multiple choice

1. 中国学生面临的最重要的考试有 ______。
   A. 小学入学考试　B. 小学升初中考试
   C. 初中升高中考试　D. 高中升大学考试
2. “应试教育”是指教师的一切教学活动和学生的一切学习活动基本上都是围绕着“ ______ ”来进行的。
   A. 素质　B. 考试　C. 体育　D. 儒家
3. “高考”是 ______ 的入学考试。
   A. 幼儿园　B. 小学　C. 大学　D. 中学
4. 美国大学 ______ 录取学生。
   A. 按照全国统一的考试成绩　B. 按照学生平时的测验成绩
   C. 按照每个学校自己的标准　D. 按照课外书
5. 采取什么样的教育制度，与一个国家的 ______、______、______ 有关。
   A. 传统文化　B. 学生数量　C. 学校数量　D. 知识结构

三、问 答 Short answer questions

1. 什么是“应试教育”？什么是“素质教育”？
   What is “exam-oriented education”? What is “quality-oriented education”?
2. 中国学生面临的最重要的考试是什么？
   What are the most important exams that Chinese students are facing?

信息链接 Information Link

http://www.yuelushuyuan.com/
http://www.huaxia.com/
http://www.pku.edu.cn/
www.blcu.edu.cn
http://www.cun.edu.cn/
http://www.edu.cn/HomePage/english/resources/universities/
http://www.answers.com/topic/guozijian-beijing
http://www.china-tour.cn/People-And-Customs/Chinese-Education.htm
http://www.e-admission.edu.cn/
http://thingschinese.wordpress.com/

资料搜集 Data Collection

岳麓书院 Yue Lu Academy

汉语拼音____

燕京大学 Yen Ching University

汉语拼音________________________________

北京大学 Peking University

汉语拼音________________________________

北京语言大学 Beijing Language and Culture University

汉语拼音________________________________

中央民族大学 Minzu University of China

汉语拼音________________________________

拓展活动
Extention

一、探索 Exploration

请简述北京国子监的历史。

Please briefly introduce the history of The Imperial Academy, Guo Zi Jian of Beijing.

二、讨论 Discussion

以后中国会取消高考吗?

Will the national matriculation examination of China be abolished later on?

三、报告 Presentation

1. 应试教育和素质教育的比较。

   The comparison between exam-oriented education and quality-oriented education.

2. 高考与SAT的比较。

   The comparison between the national matriculation examination of China and the SAT.

英语译文
English Version of the Text

Homework and tests are two important things students face usually. They are based on the different educational systems. Essentially, the education in China is mainly exam-oriented; that means all the teacher's teaching and all the students' learning serve the examination. Therefore, in Chinese schools, the homework assigned by teachers is always about the practice of the text with different degrees of difficulty. Discussion and after-school reading to extend the knowledge outside of the class will not be assigned.

The examination especially for the enrollment from junior high school to senior high school, and national matriculation examination are the most important examinations Chinese students are facing. The achievement even influence the student's whole life. National matriculation examination is considered the highest-level examination in academics worldwide. Under the exam-oriented education system, the knowledge structure of Chinese students is quite different from that of American students.

Quality-oriented education is widely applied in the United States. Different from exam-oriented education, it places more importance on the student's knowledge completeness, analysis and exploration. The homework teachers assign is basically of discussion practice and after-school reading. The examination achievement not only refers to the credit on the test paper, but also the general student performance in classes and the student's quiz marks. Another difference from China is that, there is no nationwide matriculation examination in the United States; every university matriculates the students by its own standards.

What the educational system is in a country relates to the traditional culture of that country and the quantity of students and schools. In past China, relatively short of educational resources, the exam-oriented education better fits its reality. In recent years, more attention has been paid to quality-oriented education in China, and the exam system has undergone a great change.

第二十课 我的学校

Wǒ de xuéxiào

Lesson 20 My School

在 1949 年以前，中国的学校由公立学校和私立学校组成。1949 年以后，私立学校逐步转变为由国家管理的公立学校。从 20 世纪 90 年代开始，作为对公立学校的补充，并为解决教育资源缺乏的问题，大量私立学校重新出现。另一方面，中国的职业教育也十分发达，几乎每个城市都有不同专业的技术学校。

清华大学

贵州省的一所希望小学

据统计，中国共有约 12.91 万所幼儿园、32.01 万所小学、5.94 万所初中、31, 255 所高中、2, 321 所大学，其中私立大学为 297 所。[①] 政府实施的“211

工程”和“希望工程”，对中国的高等教育和初等教育均有着明显的推动作用。中国的公立小学和初中都强制实行义务教育。

在少数民族地区，如西藏、新疆和内蒙古，除用汉语授课外，当地少数民族语言也在课堂上和教科书上使用。

一所维吾尔语小学

从欧洲人的殖民地发展到今天，美国没有像中国那样经历过从传统的私塾教育到现代教育的转变。美国的教育从一开始就继承并发展了欧洲大陆的教育模式，成为目前世界上教育水平最高的国家之一。

美国的公立中小学有 9 万所左右，占全国中小学总数的 70% 多，承担了大约 90% 中小学生的基础教育。至 2000 年，美国大学有 4096 所。其中公立四年制大学 615 所，两年制大学 1092 所；私立四年制大学 1705 所，两年制大学 684 所。私立大学的数量略高于公立大学，这一点和中国的情况很不一样。

美国的两年制公立大学也可称为社区学院，在中国没有与其相当的教育机构。社区学院在减轻学生经济负担方面起到了很大的作用。

在中国，无论公立的还是私立的中小学，开设

① 教育部 2008 年 4 月公布。

的课程基本一样，但在美国有时会有一些差别。AP课程是美国中学教育的一个特色，目前在中国还没有设立。

常春藤联盟 (Chángchūnténg Liánméng, the Ivy League) 代表着美国高等教育的最高水平。

西雅图一所社区学院的教室

成立于1636年的美国第一所私立大学——哈佛大学

词汇 Vocabulary

公立 gōnglì	public
组成 zǔchéng	be constituted of, make up of
补充 bǔchōng	supplement
缺乏 quēfá	lack, absence
重新 chóngxīn	anew, again
出现 chūxiàn	appear, emerge

职业教育 zhíyè jiàoyù	vocational education
专业 zhuānyè	speciality
统计 tǒngjì	statistics
幼儿园 yòu'éryuán	nursery, kindergarten
实施 shíshī	actualize, implement
高等 gāoděng	higher level

初等 chūděng	primary, elementary	一开始 yìkāishǐ	at the very beginning
推动 tuīdòng	promote	基础 jīchǔ	base, elements
义务教育 yìwù jiàoyù	compulsory education	相当 xiāngdāng	correspond to
殖民地 zhímíndì	colony	机构 jīgòu	organization
经历 jīnglì	experience	开设 kāishè	set up
私塾 sīshú	traditional private school		

课文理解
Understanding of the Text

一、判断 True-false questions

1. 中国的学校都是公立的。 □ 对 □ 错
2. 中国几乎每个城市都有职业技术学校。 □ 对 □ 错
3. 中国的“211 工程”是针对幼儿教育的。 □ 对 □ 错
4. 中国的“希望工程”是针对大学教育的。 □ 对 □ 错
5. 在中国的少数民族地区，学校用汉语和少数民族语言授课。 □ 对 □ 错

二、选择 Multiple choice

1. 1949年以后，中国的私立学校逐步转变为______。
   A. 社区学院　B. 公立学校　C. 教会学校　D. 技术学校
2. 据统计，中国共有约 12.91 万所______、32.01 万所______、31, 255 所______、2, 321 所______。
   A. 大学　B. 高中　C. 小学　D. 幼儿园

3. 美国的公立中小学有 9 万所左右，占全国中小学总数的 70% 多。那么全美国总共有中小学约 ______ 所，其中私立学校约有 ______ 所。
   A. 20 万　　B. 1 3 万　　C. 9 万　　D. 4 万
4. 社区学院 ______ 了美国学生的经济负担。
   A. 增加　　B. 消除　　C. 减轻　　D. 转移
5. 美国的常春藤联盟是 ______ 联盟。
   A. 幼儿园　　B. 小学　　C. 大学　　D. 中学

三、问 答 Short answer questions

查阅一下清华大学的历史，并用汉语做一个简短的介绍。
Look up the history of Tsinghua University, and briefly introduce it in Chinese.

信息链接 Information Link

http://www.project-hope.org/
http://www.cydf.org.cn/
http://www.tsinghua.edu.cn/qhdwzy/index.jsp
http://www.bfsu.edu.cn/
http://www.cbe21.com/
http://www.chinaedu.edu.cn/
http://www.jy135.com/
http://www.china.org.cn/
http://www.50states.com/college/
http://www.harvard.edu/

资料搜集
Data Collection

211工程 211 Project

汉语拼音________________________________

希望工程 The Hope Project

汉语拼音________________________________

985工程 985 Project

汉语拼音________________________________

西藏中学 Tibet Middle School

汉语拼音________________________________

拓展活动
Extention

一、探索 Exploration

填写你的教育简历表：

Fill out the form about your education resume:

姓名 Name	性别 男□ 女□ Gender M F	出生年月：__年__月__日 Date of Birth: yy/mm/dd
起止时间 Duration	学校名称 School	学历 Education Level
年至 年 Year to		
年至 年 Year to		
年至 年 Year to		
年至 年 Year to		
年至 年 Year to		

二、讨论 Discussion

根据第十六课到第二十课的课文内容，比较一下中美两国在教育上的差异。

Compare the education between China and the United States according to the texts from Lesson Sixteen to Lesson Twenty.

三、报告 Presentation

比较中美两国学生辍学（chuòxué, drop out of school）的原因。

Compare the reasons students drop out of school in China and the United States.

	中国 China	美国 USA
社会原因 Social factors		
家庭原因 Family factors		
个人原因 Personal factors		
其他原因 Other factors		

英语译文
English Version of the Text

Chinese schools were composed of public schools and private schools before 1949. Since 1949, Chinese private schools have gradually changed into public schools managed by government. However, from the 1990s until now, as a supplement for public schools, a great number of private schools have reappeared. On the other hand, vocational education has been developed very much in China; in almost every city there are vocational technology schools in different majors.

According to a recent statistics, in China, there are about 129,100 kindergartens, 320,100 elementary schools, 59,400 secondary schools, 31,255 high schools and 2,321 universities, the number of private universities is 297. The 211 Project and the Hope Project implemented by the government have improved higher education and elementary education effectively. Public schools including elementary schools and junior high schools carry out compulsory education.

In the minority areas, such as Tibet, Xinjiang and Inner Mongolia, the local minority languages are used in classrooms and textbooks besides Chinese.

From European colonies time to the present, the United States has never experienced a change from traditional private school education to modern education, as China did. The United States inherited and developed the European educational mode, and has become one of the countries whose educational level is highest in the world.

There are about 90,000 public elementary and high schools in the USA, which is 70% of the total number. 90% of students in elementary school and high school attend public school. Up until 2000, in the United States, there were 4,096 universities. Included in this are: 615 4-year public universities, 1092 2-year public colleges, 1705 4-year private universities, 684 2-year private colleges. The number of private universities and colleges is little more than public; this is quite different from China.

The 2-year public college in the United States can be called the community college. There is no any equivalent educational organization in China. Community college succeeds in decreasing student's economic burden.

In China, the courses are almost the same no matter whether they are in public elementary and high school or private school, but there is a bit of difference in the United States. The AP course is a feature of American high school education, and China has not set up this kind of course.

The Ivy League represents the highest level of American higher education.

第二十一课 街道办事处和社区委员会

Jiēdào bànshìchù hé shèqū wěiyuánhuì

Lesson 21 Subdistrict Administration and Community Committee

在中国，城市的最低一级政府是区政府，比如北京市海淀区人民政府。在海淀区内有若干社区，或叫街道，如紫竹院街道。街道办事处不属于一级政府。紫竹院街道办事处就是海淀区政府的一个派出机构。街道办事处负责当地居民的一些具体事务，如绿化、公园管理、治安、社会福利、商业管理、残疾人协助、婚姻、计划生育、就业、法律协助和市容卫生等。街道办事处还要完成区政府临时交给的任务，比如，选举时的选务安排等。至今为止，中华人民共和国共约有街道办事处 6, 686 个。

中国城市居民的生活离不开街道办事处。有些学校为了更好地管理学生的校外生活，也经常与街道办事处联系，取得他们的帮助。

北京紫竹院街道办事处在召开一个关于人口普查的会议

首先要明确的概念是，中国地方政府大体是按照省、自治区、直辖市——市、县、区——乡、镇等三级来划分的，各级政府之间是上下级的领导与被领导的关系。而美国是按照州——县——市来划分的，但各政府之间没有明显的上下级关系。由于中美两国的国情不同，历史不同，所采取的政治制度也有很大的差异。

美国的一个市里往往会有几个社区，这有些像中国的街道，社区委员会虽然与市政府有很多联系，但并不是市政府的派出机构。由于社区管理涉及社区安全、区域规划、环境保护、垃圾处理、社会福利、住房维修、妇幼保健、老人服务、社区教育等诸多方面，因此，社区委员会通常都根据本社区的实际需要把工作划分成若干方面，由专人负责，并组成专业委员会，如环境保护委员会、儿童福利委员会、教育委员会等。社区专业委员会负责人由社区委员会委员担任，其他成员则由社区居民竞选担任。

美国社区组织的健身活动

词汇 Vocabulary

街道 jiēdào	street, subdistrict
社区 shèqū	community
委员会 wěiyuánhuì	committee
派出 pàichū	expedite, send
负责 fùzé	take charge, with responsibility for
具体 jùtǐ	material, specific
绿化 lǜhuà	rivescence
治安 zhì'ān	security
残疾人 cánjírén	the disable
协助 xiézhù	assist
卫生 wèishēng	sanitation
临时 línshí	temporary
选举 xuǎnjǔ	elect, choose

选务 xuǎnwù	election affair
首先 shǒuxiān	firstly, first thing
明确 míngquè	definitude, explicit
概念 gàiniàn	concept
涉及 shèjí	deal with, relate to
区域 qūyù	region, area
规划 guīhuà	lay out, programming
环境保护 huánjìng bǎohù	environment protection
垃圾处理 lājī chǔlǐ	garbage disposal
妇幼保健 fùyòu bǎojiàn	health care for women and children
若干 ruògān	several, some
竞选 jìngxuǎn	electioneeringa, run

专有名词 Proper Nouns

海淀 Hǎidiàn	Haidian (district)
紫竹院 Zǐzhúyuàn	Zizhuyuan (region)

课文理解
Understanding of the Text

一、判 断 True-false questions

1. 中国城市最低一级政府是街道办事处。 □ 对 □ 错
2. 街道办事处负责城市居民的一些具体事务。 □ 对 □ 错
3. 中国城市居民的生活离不开街道办事处。 □ 对 □ 错
4. 街道办事处可以帮助学校管理学生的校外生活。 □ 对 □ 错
5. 美国地方政府是按照州——市——县——区来划分的。 □ 对 □ 错

二、选 择 Multiple choice

1. 中国城市最低一级政府是______。
   A. 省政府　B. 市政府　C. 县政府　D. 区政府
2. 中国北京市海淀区紫竹院街道办事处是______的派出机构。
   A. 中央政府　B. 北京市政府　C. 海淀区政府
3. 街道办事处负责当地的______、______、和______等事务。
   A. 计划生育　B. 学校教育　C. 公园管理　D. 法律协助
4. 中美两国政府设置的不同是因为两国的______不同。
   A. 国情　B. 历史　C. 政治制度　D. 管理机构
5. 美国的社区专业委员会的负责人由______担任。
   A. 总统　B. 州长　C. 市长　D. 社区委员会委员

三、问 答 Short answer questions

1. 中国的街道办事处都负责哪些事务？
   What affairs belong to Chinese subdistrict's responsibility?
2. 美国的社区委员会都负责哪些事务？
   What affairs belong to U.S. community committee's responsibility?

信息链接 Information Link

http://www.saic.gov.cn/
http://www.tax861.gov.cn/
http://www.bjgaj.gov.cn/web/
http://www.cnta.gov.cn/
http://www.bjciq.gov.cn/
http://www.bjciq.gov.cn/
http://www.chinacity.com.cn/
http://chinese.usembassy-china.org.cn/
http://www.china.com.cn/
http://www.foreignercn.com/
http://foreignersinchina.org/
http://www.livinginchina.com/
http://www.chinaguide.org/
http://www.ontheissues.org/China.htm
http://www.myheritage.org/committees/
http://www.geocities.com/classifiedforum/
http://www.china.com.cn/ch-zhengzhi/index.htm

资料搜集 Data Collection

工商局 Industrial and Commercial Bureau

汉语拼音________________________________

地方税务局 Local Taxation Bureau

汉语拼音____

公安局 Public Security Bureau

汉语拼音____

出入境检疫局 Entry & Exit Inspection and Quarantine Bureau

汉语拼音____

城管局 Urban Management Bureau

汉语拼音____

拓展活动 Extention

一、探索 Exploration

请查一查下面美国驻华使领馆的地址，以及这个地址在哪个街道办事处的管辖地域。在空白中国地图上标出它们所在的城市。

Please look up the addresses of the U.S. Embassy and U.S. Consulates, and what territories of the subdistrict administration office they are located in. Write them in the blank map of China below.

	地址 Address	街道办事处 Subdistrict Administration Office
北京大使馆 Beijing Embassy		
成都领事馆 Chengdu Consulate		
沈阳领事馆 Shenyang Consulate		
广州领事馆 Guangzhou Consulate		
上海总领事馆 Shanghai General Consulate		
武汉领事馆 Wuhan Consulate		

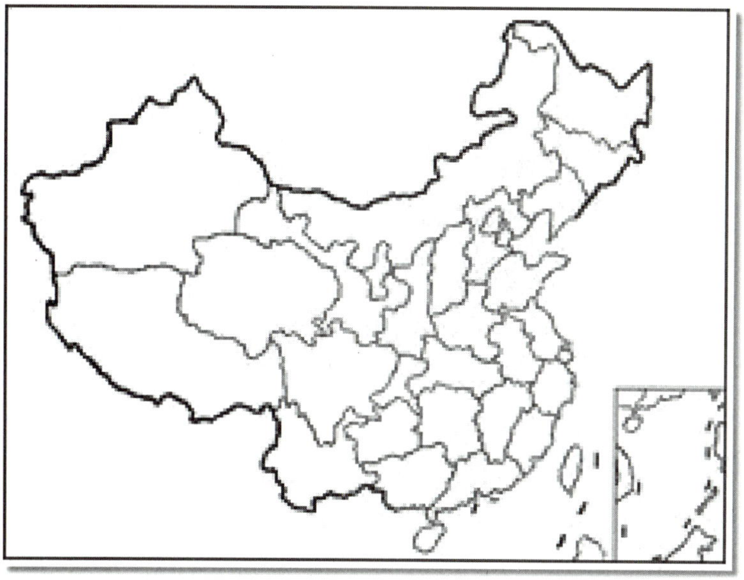

二、讨论 Discussion

当你在中国遇到下列情况时，应该怎么办？

If you met with the situation described below, what would you do?

1. 咨询并办理开设公司的手续。

   Consult with someone about the procedure of establishing a Chinese enterprise.

2. 办理结婚手续。

   Transact a marriage procedure.

3. 上学。

   Go to school.

4. 咨询旅游景点的情况。

   Consult on the condition of a scenery spot.

5. 遇到抢劫或偷盗。

   Be robbed or stolen from.

6. 遇到交通事故。

   In a traffic accident.

7. 租房（不是宾馆）。

   Rent an apartment (not hotel).

8. 找工作。

   Look for a job.

9. 签证过期。
   Visa expires.
10. 给政府提建议或意见。
   Give a suggestion or complaint to the government.
11. 发生火灾、重病等意外紧急情况。
   Emergency such as fire, serious disease occurs.
12. 丢失护照。
   Passport is lost.

三、报告 Presentation

中国街道办事处和美国社区委员会的比较。

The comparison between the subdistrict office in China and the community committee in the United States.

英语译文 English Version of the Text

In China, the lowest rank of government in the city is a district government, for example, the People's Government of Haidian District in Beijing. There are several communities or so-called subdistricts in the Haidian District, for instance, Zizhuyuan Subdistrict. The subdistrict is not in a government rank. Zizhuyuan Subdistrict Affairs Office is an organization expedited by the Haidian District government. The office is in charge of the local resident affairs, such as planting trees, park management, security, social welfare, business management, assistance for the disabled, marriage, family planning, obtaining employment, legal assistance, city maintenance and sanitation, and so on. The subdistrict also needs to complete the task assigned by the district government temporarily, for example, arranging the elections in an election year. Until now, there are about 6,686 subdistrict affair offices in the mainland of the People's Republic of China.

The town residents of China cannot live without a subdistrict affairs office. Some schools often contact it for assistance in managing students after school.

First, this concept must be clear that the administration of China is implemented in about three ranks: province/autonomous region/municipality; city/county/district; village/town, etc.The relation among them is of leading or being led according to the higher or lower rank. However, in the United States, whose administration also is implemented in three levels: state - county - city. There is no any clear relationship of higher and lower ranks. Due to the differences in background and history of China and the United States, the political system is quite different.

There are several communities in a city in the United States, somewhat like China's subdistrict. The community committee has much to do with the city government, but it is not a expedited organization. Because the community management relates to community security, region planning, environment protection, garbage disposal, social welfare, residence maintenance, health care for women and children, service for the aged, community education and so on, the community committee usually assigns a specific person to take charge of the actual needs and set up a specific committee, such as an environment protection committee, child welfare committee, education committee, etc. The head of the specific community committee must be one of the members of the community committee; the other members are elected from the residents in this community.

22

Nóngmín

第二十二课 农民

Lesson 22 Peasant

中国的十三亿人口中，农民有八亿，占人口总数的一半还多。要解决好中国的问题，首先就要解决好农民的问题。以下是中国目前所面临的“三农问题”：一、表现为农民收入低，增收难，城乡居民贫富差距大，实质表现为农民权利得不到保障的“农民问题”；二、集中表现为农村面貌落后，经济不发达，基础建设不足等，形象比喻为中国的“城市像欧洲，农村像非洲”的“农村问题”；三、集中表现为农民种田不赚钱，产业化程度低的“农业问题”。

中国最富裕的农村之一——华西村

河北省某农村村舍

在“三农问题”中，“农民问题”是核心问题。随着农村的变化和进步，很多农民，特别是青年农民，离开了土地，到城里打工，这些人被称为“农民工”。他们在城里的工厂、商店、餐馆等地方工作。大量的农民工进城，也带来了婚姻、医疗保险、子女入学等城市社会问题。因此，只关心中国的城市问题，而不关心中国的农民问题，就不可能更好地了解中国。同时，在中国，富裕地区的“三农问题”和贫穷地区的“三农问题”也不完全一样。

进城找工作的农民工

南京市的一所农民工子弟学校

美国是当今世界粮仓，是当之无愧的农业大国。然而，美国又是个农民很少的国家，其农民只占国民总数的 3% 左右。没有到过中国农村的美国人，很

难理解中文里“农村”的意思。中国的农村可以理解为村庄，由不同的家庭集中居住。这些家庭大部分存在血缘关系。而在中国人的心目中，美国的农村就是私人种植园或私人牧场，也就是说一个家庭拥有一大片土地或草场。

美国的农民家庭也许远离城市，没有太多的娱乐设施，但他们依然可以通过电视、互联网和报纸了解外面的世界。如果他们或他们的子女到城市工作的话，就可以了解更多外面的世界。私人农场主会雇佣一些人为他们工作。这些人也可以被称为是“美国的农民工”，但他们所面临的问题，与中国的农民工有相似的地方，也有不同的地方。

美国的一所农场

墨西哥籍的“农民工”

词 汇
Vocabulary

增收 zēngshōu	increase income
贫富差距 pín fù chājù	difference between the poor and the rich
权利 quánlì	right, authority
面貌 miànmào	visage
落后 luòhòu	draggle, developing, behindhand
建设 jiànshè	build, construct
不足 bùzú	deficiency, shortage
形象 xíngxiàng	image,visualize
比喻 bǐyù	figure of speech, parable
种田 zhòng tián	farm, follow the plough
赚钱 zhuàn qián	make money
农业 nóngyè	agriculture

核心 héxīn	core
进步 jìnbù	progress
打工 dǎ gōng	temp, arbeiter
粮仓 liángcāng	barn
当之无愧 dāng zhī wú kuì	fully deserve
血缘 xuèyuán	consanguinity
心目 xīnmù	memory, mind
种植园 zhòngzhíyuán	plantation
牧场 mùchǎng	pasture
草场 cǎochǎng	grassland
设施 shèshī	establishment
雇佣 gùyōng	employ

课文理解
Understanding of the Text

一、判 断 True-false questions

1. 中国有十亿农民。 □对 □错
2. “农业问题”是“三农问题”之一。 □对 □错
3. “农村问题”是“三农问题”中的核心问题。 □对 □错
4. 到城里打工的农民被称为“农民工”。 □对 □错
5. 中美两国的“农民工”面临的问题完全一样。 □对 □错

二、选 择 Multiple choice

1. “三农问题”指 ______，______ 和 ______。
   A. 农业问题　B. 农村问题　C. 农民工问题　D. 农民问题
2. “农民收入低，增收难，城乡居民贫富差距大，实质表现为农民权利得不到保障”是“三农问题”中的 ______。
   A. 农业问题　B. 农民问题　C. 农村问题　D. 农民工问题
3. “三农问题”中的核心问题是 ______。
   A. 农业问题　B. 农村问题　C. 农民工问题　D. 农民问题
4. 大量农民工进城带来的社会问题是 ______。
   A. 婚姻　B. 医疗保险　C. 子女入学　D. 粮食不够吃
5. 中美两国农村的共同特点是 ______。
   A. 都有很多家庭集中居住　B. 都有私人种植园或私人牧场
   C. 农民占国民总数的比例都很高　D. 都以农业生产为主

三、问 答 Short answer questions

1. 中国的农民工大量进城带来哪些问题？你认为应该怎么解决？
   What kind of problems does it bring up that a large number of Chinese peasants leave their fields to work in town? How to solve those problems?
2. 中国的农村与美国的农村有什么不同？
   What are the differences between villages in China and USA?

信息链接
Information Link

http://www.yangliuqingnianhua.com/
http://www.zjktour.gov.cn/GB/zjkwh/mswh/2651.shtml
http://www.laranwang.com/
http://www.artcn.cn/
http://www.56china.net/
http://www.ok0471.com/
http://www.huaxia-ng.com/
http://www.farmer.gov.cn/
http://www.nnn.net.cn/HomePage/Index.aspx
http://www.jgny.net/nong/
http://www.ourchinese.org/
http://www.bls.gov/
http://www.chinesefolkart.com/
http://www.interactchina.com/servlet/StoreFront
http://www.unpo.org/
http://www.chinaethniccrafts.com/

资料搜集
Data Collection

退耕还林 Conversion of Cropland to Forest

汉语拼音____

村村通 Installing Radio and TV in Each Village

汉语拼音____________________________________

家电下乡 Home Appliances to Rural Areas

汉语拼音____________________________________

文化下乡 Cultural Activities to Rural Areas

汉语拼音____________________________________

农机站 Farm Machinery Station

汉语拼音____________________________________

拓展活动
Extention

一、探索 Exploration

中国农民文化是中国文化的一个重要组成部分。下面的图片有的既是中国传统农民艺术作品，又是他们的日常生活用品。请在图片下填写它们的名称：
The culture of the Chinese peasant is a very important part of Chinese culture. The pictures below are either some traditional art works by Chinese peasants or their daily life articles. Please write their names underneath the pictures:

天津杨柳青______（汉族）
Yangliuqing, Tianjin (Han Nationality)

河北蔚县______（汉族）
Yuxian County, Hebei Province (Han Nationality)

广西______（壮族）
Guangxi Province (Zhuang Nationality)

云南大理______（白族）
Dali, Yunnan Province (Bai Nationality)

二、讨论 Discussion

前几年，中国的猪肉价格十分不稳定。市场上猪肉供应少了，农民就加紧养猪，但过了一段时间，由于产量过大，猪肉供应超过了市场需求，猪肉价格又降下来，甚至导致农民亏本。不仅仅是猪肉价格，其他的农产品的价格也有这样的问题。这个问题应该如何解决？

The price of pork changed very much in the last few years. When there is a lack of supply of pork in the market, peasants will press on with raising pigs. Due to the overproduction, the pork supply exceeds the market need. After a period of time, the price will lower, even drive peasants to lose a profit in the selling. This does not just happen with the pork price; the same thing happens with other agricultural products. How should this issue be solved?

三、报告 Presentation

中国农民工和美国农业工人的比较。

The comparison between peasant workers of China and the agricultural workers of the United States.

英语译文
English Version of the Text

There are eight hundred million peasants among 13 billion people in China, taking more than half of the general population. To solve the problems in China, the first thing is to solve the problems of peasants successfully. The following are the three problems, called the San Nong Issues. First issue, is represented by peasants' low income, difficulty in increasing income, big gap between the rural poor and the urban rich, and the real fact that peasants' rights are not actually guaranteed. Second issue, is represented mainly by underdevelopment in economy, deficient infrastructure and so on. There is a saying: the cities in China can be compared to the cities in Europe while the countryside in China looks like the countryside in Africa. Third issue, is represented by the fact that peasants cannot make money from planting and the agriculture industrialization is at a low level.

Among the San Nong Issues, the first one is critical. With the changes and progress in China's countryside, a large number of Chinese peasants, especially the young peasants, leave their fields to work in town; they are called peasant workers. They work in the factories, stores and restaurants of the town. The amount of peasant workers in the town bring some urban social problems, such as marriage, medicare, and their children's education. Therefore, only paying attention to cities in China, and neglecting the problems of peasants can not make you understand China better. In China, the San Nong Issues are different between the rich and the poor regions.

The United States is the world barn and fully deserved to be called a great agricultural country. Nevertheless, she is a country with few peasants, taking only about 3% of the total. For an American who has never been to the countryside of China, it is hard to understand the meaning of the Chinese word, Countryside. It can be understood as a village being composed of different families. Most of families are relatives. Chinese people think, the countryside in the United States could be a private plantation or pasture, which means a family owns a large land or grassland.

In the United States, the farmer's residence may be far away from the town, and there is little entertainment, but they can know of the outside world by TV programs, internet and newspaper. If they or their children go to work in a town, they will know more. The farmer can employ some workers. They can be called American farm workers. However, like Chinese peasant workers, the farm workers are facing some problems too. Some problems are the same, but others are not.

第二十三课 选举
Xuǎnjǔ

Lesson 23 Elections

在中国历史上，政府官员的任用大致经过了三个阶段，即隋朝（581—618）以前的推举制，隋朝至清朝（1616—1911）的科举制和1912年以后的选举制。由于历史发展不同于世界上其他国家，中国选举制度的制定和执行与其他国家也有所不同。中国的选举制度是由国情决定的。

根据中国的宪法，国家的一切权力属于人民，人民行使国家权力的机关是人民代表大会，人民代表大会代表由民主选举产生，代表人民的根本利益。

另外，中国城市和农村的基层组织机构——居民委员会和村民委员会也是由民主选举产生的。

中国有8亿农民，与城市居民相比，总体上来讲，他们的生活水平、受教育程度等都相对较低，因此，作为世界上规模最大的农民群体选举——村民委员会选举和以城市居民为基础的社区居民委员会选举可能会有一些区别。

虽然有一些需要继续完善的地方，但目前中国所实行的选举制度是符合中国国情的，并且充分表达了中国人民的意愿。

中国封建社会在1911年结束以后，无论中华民国时期，还是中华人民共和国时期，一个大党执政，

（左）村民委员会选举
（右）居民委员会选举

并和若干小党共存是中国的基本政治局面，从没出现过政党轮替执政的情况。这是中国历史、文化和国情所决定的。所以，以两党制和组阁制为基础的选举制度在中国没有深厚而广泛的历史、社会和政治依据。

美国建国之初，乔治·华盛顿等政治家参考并继承了欧洲大陆的选举体制，并结合美国刚刚从殖民地社会解放出来的现实，制定了美国的选举制度，并得到了大多数美国人民的认可和拥护。由此可以看出，一个国家的选举制度必须既要有历史文化依据，又要合乎本国的现实情况。

与中国的选举不同，美国不存在数字庞大的农民选民。在“两党制”的政党轮替执政中，是共和党执政，还是民主党执政，是美国选举的最核心内容或目的。

另一个与中国选举的最大不同是，两党的候选人背后都有不同的组织、企业或个人进行经济方面的资助，并有专业人士对候选人的政治纲领进行策划，甚至对候选人的宣传，包括语言、动作、服装、化妆等进行设计。候选人和他的竞选团队在选举期间的出色表现，会给民众十分深刻的印象。

无论哪种选举制度，都是从这个国家自己的历史文化演变而来的，都是这个国家大多数人民的选择。

（左）奥巴马和麦凯恩竞选时的场景
（右）投票

词汇 Vocabulary

大致 dàzhì	approximately
阶段 jiēduàn	moment, phase
推举制 tuījǔzhì	recommendation system
科举制 kējǔzhì	imperial examination system
执行 zhíxíng	carry out, implement
人民代表大会 rénmín dàibiǎo dàhuì	the people's congress
规模 guīmó	scale, size
群体 qúntǐ	group
局面 júmiàn	complexion, phase
轮替 lúntì	rotation
组阁制 zǔgézhì	organize-the-cabinet system
深厚 shēnhòu	profundity, deep
广泛 guǎngfàn	abroad

体制 tǐzhì	system
解放 jiěfàng	liberate
认可 rènkě	approbate, recognize
候选人 hòuxuǎnrén	candidate
资助 zīzhù	imburse
纲领 gānglǐng	creed
策划 cèhuà	mastermind
宣传 xuānchuán	propaganda
团队 tuánduì	team
深刻 shēnkè	profundity, deeply
印象 yìnxiàng	impression
演变 yǎnbiàn	involvement, outcome

专有名词 Proper Nouns

隋朝 Suí Cháo	Sui Dynasty	共和党 Gònghé Dǎng	the Republican
中华民国 Zhōnghuá Mínguó	Republic of China	民主党 Mínzhǔ Dǎng	the Democrat
乔治·华盛顿 Qiáozhì Huáshèngdùn	Geroge Washington		

课文理解 Understanding of the Text

一、判断 True-false questions

1. 中国从隋朝时开始实行“科举制”。 □对 □错
2. 人民代表大会是选举机构。 □对 □错
3. 中国的村民委员会选举是城市居民参加的选举。 □对 □错
4. “两党制”和“组阁制”不适合中国的现实情况。 □对 □错
5. 在美国“民主党”和“共和党”轮替执政。 □对 □错

二、选择 Multiple choice

1. 中国在隋朝以前，政府通过 ______ 制任用官员。
   A. 科举　B. 推举　C. 选举
2. 从隋朝到清朝，政府通过 ______ 制任用官员。
   A. 选举　B. 科举　C. 推举
3. 1912 年以后，中国采取了 ______ 制。
   A. 科举　B. 推举　C. 选举
4. 世界上规模最大的农民选举是 ______。
   A. 英国大选　B. 美国大选　C. 中国农民村委会选举　D. 德国大选

5.“两党制”和“组阁制”为基础的选举制度在中国没有深厚而广泛的 ______、______ 和 ______ 依据。

A. 社会　　B. 历史　　C. 政治　　D. 教育

三、问答 Short answer questions

1. 为什么说中国村民委员会选举是世界上最大的农民群体选举？
Why is it said that the election for villager committee in China is the biggest peasant-group election in the world?

2. 为什么中国不适合“两党制”和“组阁制”？
Why can both two-party system and organizing-the-cabinet system not be realized in China?

信息链接 Information Link

http://www.npc.gov.cn
http://www.cppcc.gov.cn/
http://www.taimeng.org.cn/
http://www.dem-league.org.cn/
http://www.kmt.org.tw/
http://www.wengewang.org/
http://www.chinareform.net/
http://www.chinaelections.org/
http://www.dxscg.cn/
http://www.cartercenter.org/homepage.html
http://www.world-china.org/

资料搜集
Data Collection

全国人民代表大会 The National People's Congress of the People's Republic of China

汉语拼音____________________

中国人民政治协商会议 The Chinese People's Political Consultative Conference

汉语拼音____________________

中国共产党 The Communist Party of China

汉语拼音____________________

八大民主党派 Eight Democratic Parties

汉语拼音____

中华人民共和国宪法
Constitution of the People's Republic of China

汉语拼音____

选举法
The Electoral Law

汉语拼音____

拓展活动
Extention

一、探索 Exploration

请查阅什么是中国的八大民主党派。他们与中国的民主进程有什么关系？
Please look up the Eight Democratic Parties of China, and their relationship with the democratic progress of China.

二、讨论 Discussion

目前很多中国大学生通过竞争去当农村干部——“村官”。作为就业的一个途径，社会上对这一现象评价不一。那么你对这个问题有什么看法呢？
Nowadays, lots of Chinese students are competing to be a village cadre, village official. As an approach to obtain employment, the phenomenon is commented on differently. What is your opinion about it?

三、报告 Presentation

中国村民委员会选举与社区居民委员会选举的异同。
The difference between the election of villager committee and community committee.

英语译文
English Version of the Text

In Chinese history, the appointment of governmental officials has three phases approximately, namely the recommendation system before the Sui Dynasty (AD 581 - 618), the imperial examination system from the Sui Dynasty to the Qing Dynasty (AD 1616- 1912), and the election system from 1912 to the present. Compared to the history from other countries, the constitution and implementation of Chinese election is different. The election system is determined by the national conditions of China.

According to the China's constitution, all the power of state belongs to the people, the people's congress is an organization whereby people execute state power, and the representatives of the people's congress are elected through democratic election, representing the fundamental will of the people.

Meanwhile, the local organizations in China cities and villages—community committee and villager committee are also elected through democratic election.

China has eight hundred million peasants, compared to the town residents; both of their living conditions and education are lower. Therefore, with the biggest peasant-group voters, the election for villager committee can't be the same as the one for the community committee based on town residents in form and content.

Although some components of the Chinese election still need to be perfected continuously, the current election system corresponds to the Chinese condition and personal desire of the people.

Since 1911, the end of Chinese feudalism system, no matter whether in a period of Republic of China or People's Republic of China, the concomitant of a big party and several small parties has been a basic political complexion; the rotating reign of parties has never happened. The election system based on a two-party system and organizing-the-cabinet system has no deep foundation in history, society and politics of China.

At the beginning of the foundation of the United States, George Washington and other politicians consulted and inherited the election system of the European continent, and combined with the reality that the United States was just liberated from a colonial society, they constituted the election system of the United States, and achieved approbation and support from the people. It is found in the United States that the election system of a country not only must be based on the history and culture, but fits the real condition of the country.

Different from the election in China, in the Unites States there is no such a great number of peasant voters. In the rotating reign of two parties, whether the party in power is the Republican or the Democrat is the core and content of election of the United States.

Another difference from the Chinese system, is that the candidates from the two parties are compensated economically by various organizations, enterprises and individuals. The political creed of a candidate is masterminded by the specialists, and propaganda for a candidate is designed, including his language, motions, clothes and make-up. The outstanding performance of a candidate and his team will impress the people deeply.

No matter which election system, it is surely the outcome of the history and culture of the country,and the choice of most people in the country.

Gònghé yǔ liánbāng

第二十四课 共和与联邦

Lesson 24 Republic and Federation

中华人民共和国成立的时候，未来的国家领导人们曾经与其他政治家和学者讨论过这样一个话题：中国应该采取共和制还是联邦制？最后的结论是采取共和制。因为，第一，在中国五千多年的历史中，统一是社会发展的主流，分裂往往给人民带来灾难；第二，从当时的社会情况看，第二次世界大战和三年内战刚刚结束，边疆地区的局势还不是特别稳定，经济重建又需要中央政府在行政方面的统一领导，所以，采取更利于维护国家统一的共和制得到了当时大多数政治家和学者的赞同，也反映了大多数中国人民的愿望。

在一个统一的多民族国家内，由于宗教、经济

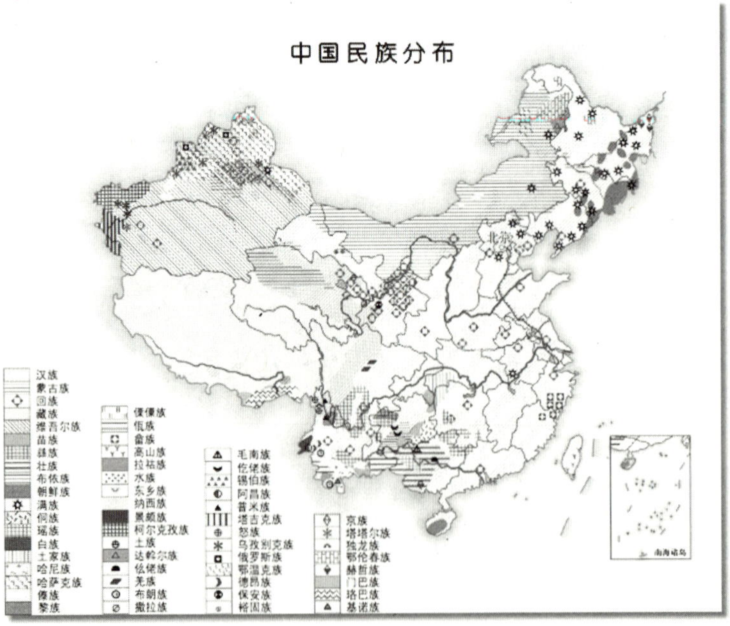

和政治等原因，有时可能会产生破坏国家统一的分裂主义势力和分裂主义分子。但他们的观点并不能代表全体人民，甚至不能代表他们本民族中大多数人的利益。他们有些过激的分裂主义行为，甚至直接转化成了恐怖主义活动。其实，世界上无论哪个国家，也无论实行共和制还是联邦制，都决不会允许分裂国家的行为发生。

2008年北京奥运会期间，天安门广场上的民族团结柱

1607年到1753年，是美洲的殖民时期，英国、法国、西班牙等欧洲各国的殖民者在美洲划分了各自的领地。由于英国殖民者与他们的宗主国英国在政治、经济上的矛盾，从1775年1783年，他们展开了脱离英国统治的“独立运动”，经过战争，美国宣告独立。19世纪初期，美国继续向西扩张，从包括原始13个州的联邦国家，发展成为具有更多州参加的联邦国家，版图从大西洋沿岸扩展到了太平洋沿岸。1861年至1865年期间，由于南方各州与北方各州在政治、经济，甚至某些思想上的分歧，宣布脱离联邦，另组政府，这引起了长达4年的南北战争，最后北方胜利，美国再次统一。从美国二百多年的历史来看，联邦制下的统一，是美国政治家和

大多数美国人民的共同愿望。

同中国一样，美国也是一个多族群的国家，族群之间的矛盾，也是不可避免的问题。但是，如果某些独立组织真的使用暴力手段以达到脱离联邦的目的，也必将会遭到政府和广大人民的坚决反对。

去教会是很多美国人日常生活的一个重要内容

词 汇
Vocabulary

学者 xuézhě	scholar
共和制 gònghézhì	republic
联邦制 liánbāngzhì	federation
结论 jiélùn	conclusion
主流 zhǔliú	mainstream
分裂 fēnliè	abruption
灾难 zāinàn	disaster
内战 nèizhàn	civil war
边疆 biānjiāng	border
局势 júshì	situation
分裂主义 fēnliè zhǔyì	splittism
利益 lìyì	benefit
恐怖主义 kǒngbù zhǔyì	terrorism
划分 huàfēn	measure off, compartmentalize
宗主国 zōngzhǔguó	suzerain
展开 zhǎnkāi	deploy, out spread

脱离 tuōlí	break away, deviate
独立 dúlì	independence
宣告 xuāngào	declare, pronounce
扩张 kuòzhāng	dilatation, expand
分歧 fēnqí	bifurcation, divarication

专有名词 Proper Nouns

第二次世界大战 Dì Èr Cì Shìjiè Dàzhàn	the World War II
南北战争 Nán-Běi Zhànzhēng	War between the States

课文理解 Understanding of the Text

一、判断 True-false questions

1. 中国是联邦制国家。 □ 对 □ 错
2. 统一是中国历史发展的主流。 □ 对 □ 错
3. 共和制更有利于中国的国家建设。 □ 对 □ 错
4. 分裂主义分子的观点不能代表全体中国人民。 □ 对 □ 错
5. 美国是一个共和制的国家。 □ 对 □ 错

二、选择 Multiple choice

1. 中国采取共和制的原因是：______。
   A. 边疆需要稳定局势 B. 苏联要求中国采取共和制
   C. 美国希望中国采取共和制 D. 中国历史上社会发展的主流是统一
2. 在一个统一的多民族国家内，由于______、______和______等原因，有时候可能会产生分裂主义分子。
   A. 宗教 B. 经济 C.教育 D.政治

3. 美国“独立战争”发生于______。
   A. 1607年　B. 1753年　C. 1775年　D. 1783年

4. 美国“南北战争”发生的原因是：______。
   A. 南方各州宣布脱离联邦　B. 南方各州宣布加入联邦
   C. 北方要求南方独立　D. 北方要求南方参加战争

三、问 答 Short answer questions

1. 中国为什么选择共和制？
   Why does China choose to implement the republic?
2. 为什么会产生分裂主义？
   What brings division?

信息链接 Information Link

http://www.huaxia.com/xjbt/index.html
http://www.mzb.com.cn/
http://www.hwjyw.com/
http://www.5i6you.cn/
http://www.yonghegong.cn/
http://www.c-c-c.org/
http://www.paulnoll.com/China/Minorities/China-min-policy.html
http://www.seac.gov.cn/gjmw/index.htm
http://www.newspiritualbible.com/
http://eng.tibet.cn/
http://www.tibettravel.org/
http://www.youxizang.com/
http://www.silkroadcn.com/
http://www.infoplease.com/
http://www.chinaxinjiang.cn/

资料搜集
Data Collection

苏公塔 Eminhezhuo Memorial Tower

汉语拼音______________________________

新疆伊犁林则徐纪念馆
Lin Zexun Memorial House in Yili, Xinjiang

汉语拼音______________________________

包尔汉 Borhan

汉语拼音______________________________

马良骏大阿訇 Imam Ma Junliang

汉语拼音____

雍和宫 Yonghe Palace

汉语拼音____

西藏大学 University of Tibet

汉语拼音____

十世班禅大师 Master Banchan of 10th Generation

汉语拼音____

拓展活动
Extention

一、探索 Exploration

请说明什么叫中国的“民族区域自治”。

Please comment on the national regional autonomy of China.

二、讨论 Discussion

在学习维吾尔语的同时学习汉语，会影响维吾尔族文化的继承和发展吗？

Will it influence the heritage and development of Uigur culture learning Uigur while learning Chinese?

三、报告 Presentation

美国废除奴隶制和西藏废除农奴制的比较。

The comparison between the slavery system abolishment in the United States and Tibet.

英语译文
English Version of the Text

When the People's Republic of China was founded, the future national leaders and other politicians and scholars always talked about the following topic: Will China implement a republic or a federation? The final conclusion was to implement the republic, because, first, during Chinese history for five thousand years, unification has been the mainstream of social development, and separation always brought disaster to the Chinese people; Second, because of the condition of that time, when World War II and the three-year Civil War had just ended, the situation on the border was not very peaceful. Consolidated leadership and arrangement of central government were required to recover the economy. Therefore, the republic, which supports the country's unification, was approved by most of politicians and scholars; it also reflected the desire of most Chinese people.

In an unified country with multiple ethnic groups, it is possible to produce division for the issues of religion, economy and politics. But their viewpoint cannot represent all Chinese people, even most people from their own ethnic group. Some extremists' ultra division will be transformed into terrorism activities. In fact, no matter which government in the world, the republic or the federation, both will be strongly against splitting the country.

From 1607 to 1753, the United States was in her immigration period; English, French, Spanish and other European colonists measured off territory of their own. Due to the political and economic contradiction between English colonists and their reigning Britain, from 1775 to 1783, they began the Independent movement to separate from the British government, and declared the establishment of the United States of America. In the early 19th century, America expanded westward continuously, and became a federative country with more states from the beginning of the original thirteen states. The territory reached the Pacific coast from the Atlantic coast. From 1861 to 1865, because of the bifurcation and contradiction between the South and the North in politics, economics and ideology, the South declare its independence and built another government. This led to a four-year war between the states; finally, the North won, and the United States unified again. Looking at American history for two hundred years, unification under a federation is the common desire of American politicians and most of the people.

Just as China, the United States is a multiple-raced country. The contradiction between races is an unavoidable phenomenon. Nevertheless, if a divisive organization carried out a violation to realize independence, they will be beaten back by the government and most of the people.

25

Zhànzhēng yǔ hépíng

第二十五课 战争与和平

Lesson 25 War and Peace

在中国五千年的历史中，经历了无数次战争。所有这些战争，可以概括为两种类型：一种是中国人自己内部的战争——内战；一种是抵御外国侵略的抗战。中国人，特别是占人口绝大多数的汉族人，几乎没有主动发起过打击、掠夺其他民族的侵略战争，这并不是因为汉民族不够强大，而是因为在汉民族的文化中，儒家“和”的观念深刻影响了人们的思想。但汉民族并不惧怕战争，而且从长期的战争中总结出了智慧的战争艺术，《孙子兵法》就是一个实例。

支援中国抗战的美国“飞虎队”队员

在现代历史上，中国有四次较大规模的出境作战，即第二次世界大战期间，1942 年中国军队进入缅甸（Miǎndiàn, Myanmar）抗击日本侵略者的作战、1950 年到 1953 年的朝鲜战争（Cháoxiǎn Zhànzhēng,

朝鲜战争中，交战双方交换战俘

Korea War）、1962 年的中印边境战争 (Zhōng-Yìn Biānjìng Zhànzhēng, the Border War between China and India) 和 1979 年的中越战争 (Zhōng-Yuè Zhànzhēng, China-Vietnam War)。

第二次世界大战时，中美两国军队是盟友；而朝鲜战争时，两国军队则互相为敌。就战争而言，可以从不同的角度去分析，并作出结论。但无论如何，更重要的是总结历史，面向未来。

1979年邓小平访美

在美国二百多年的历史上，先后进行了独立战争、南北内战、美墨战争（Měi-Mò Zhànzhēng, America-Mexico War）、美西战争 (Měi-Xī Zhànzhēng, America-Spain War)，以及包括第一次世界大战和第二次世界大战在内的二百多次大大小小的海外战争。这些频繁的战争并不能说明美国人民不热爱和平。正是由于美国参加了欧洲战场和亚洲战场的反法西斯战争，才使得世界和平能够尽快到来，并也使得美国成为那时世界和平的主要缔造者之一。

美国国内和世界其他各国的政治家对美国所参加的一些战争都有不同的理解和评价，包括美国人民在内的世界各国人民也对一些战争有着不同的看法。从总体上来看，每次战争的发动都与政治、经济、意识形态等有着密切的联系。2003 年到 2010 年的伊拉克（Yīlākè, Iraq）战争、2001 年开始的阿富汗 (Āfùhàn, Afghanistan) 战争等，也都是由这些原因引起的。

美国人民的和平愿望，其他国家的国家利益和美国国家利益的矛盾，以及美国政治家对美国利益的保护及决策，时刻影响着美国乃至全世界的战争与和平。从历史和文化的角度来研究中国和美国在战争观上的区别，是一项十分有意义的工作。

词汇 Vocabulary

概括 gàikuò	summary, sum up
抵御 dǐyù	fight back
外国 wàiguó	foreign country
抗战 kàngzhàn	war resistance against aggression
主动 zhǔdòng	initiatively
掠夺 lüèduó	grab
侵略 qīnlüè	invade
智慧 zhìhuì	wisdom
实例 shílì	example
作战 zuòzhàn	campaign, do battle

抗击 kàngjī	combat, fight
盟友 méngyǒu	ally
战场 zhànchǎng	battlefield
缔造者 dìzàozhě	creator, establisher
评价 píngjià	appraise, estimate
总体 zǒngtǐ	colletivity, general
意识形态 yìshi xíngtài	ideology
决策 juécè	decision-making
时刻 shíkè	the time of day, moment

专有名词 Proper Nouns

孙子兵法 Sūnzǐ Bīngfǎ	Sun Zi Strategics
日本 Rìběn	Japan
独立战争 Dúlì Zhànzhēng	the Independence War

第一次世界大战 Dì Yī Cì Shìjiè Dàzhàn	the World War I
法西斯 Fǎxīsī	Fascism

课文理解
Understanding of the Text

一、判 断 True-false questions

1. 内战是中国战争史上的一种常见形式。 □对 □错
2. 儒家“和”的观念深刻影响了汉民族的思想。 □对 □错
3.《孙子兵法》是一部经济学著作。 □对 □错
4. 第二次世界大战时，中国和美国是敌人。 □对 □错
5. 美国人民和中国人民一样热爱和平。 □对 □错

二、选 择 Multiple choice

1. 在中国五千年的历史中，所有的战争基本可以分为 ______、______ 两类。
   A. 抗战　B. 内战　C. 心理战　D. 信息战
2. 中国人，特别是占人口绝大多数的汉族人，______ 主动发起过打击、掠夺其他民族的侵略战争。
   A. 经常　B. 几乎没有
3. 儒家“______”的观念深刻影响了汉民族的思想。
   A. 战　B. 礼　C. 和　D. 仁
4. ______ 是中国古代著名的军事家。
   A. 孟子　B. 孙子　C. 孔子　D. 老子
5. 正是由于美国参加了欧洲战场和亚洲战场的反 ________ 战争，才使得世界和平能够尽快到来。
   A. 社会主义　B. 资本主义　C. 恐怖主义　D. 法西斯

三、问 答 Short answer questions

1. 中国历史上战争的两种类型是什么？
   What are the two types of wars in the Chinese history?
2. 在哪场战争中，中美两国是盟军？在哪场战争中，中美两国又是敌人？
   In which war were the armies of China and U.S. allies? And in which war enemies of one another?

信息链接
Information Link

http://www.sonofthesouth.net/texas/independence-movement.htm
http://www.texasnationalist.com/
http://www.harvardsquarelibrary.org/cfs/john_king_fairbank.php
http://www.warbirdforum.com/clc.htm
http://www.answers.com/topic/john-leighton-stuart
http://www.bookrags.com/wiki/John_Leighton_Stuart
http://www.china1931.cn/Index.html
http://www.hxlsw.com/
http://www.wenbao.net/
http://hist.cersp.com/
http://www.visualstatistics.net/
http://www-chaos.umd.edu/history/toc.html
http://www.chinapage.com/history1.html

资料搜集
Data Collection

费正清 Fairbank John King

汉语拼音____

埃德加·斯诺 Snow Edgar

汉语拼音________________________________

安格尼斯·史沫特莱 Smedley Agnes

汉语拼音________________________________

哈佛燕京研究院 Yenching Institute, Harvard University

汉语拼音________________________________

陈纳德 Claire Lee Chennalt

汉语拼音________________________________

司徒雷登 John Leighton Stuart

汉语拼音___________________________

拓展活动
Extention

一、探索 Exploration

课文里说："中国人，特别是占人口绝大多数的汉族人，几乎没有主动发起过打击、掠夺其他民族的侵略战争……"这句话的意思是，汉民族发起对外战争的原因主要是抵抗外来侵略。你认为这句话对不对？如果你认为不对，请你找出史实来说明一个例外。

It is said in the text that Chinese, especially Han Nationality with the great majority in total chinese population, seldom or never start a war initially to strike or rob other nationalities. These words mean that the main reasons why Chinese Hans started foreign wars is to fight back the invasion. If you think this is not true, please find out a historical truth that is an exception.

二、讨论 Discussion

为什么说2008年拉萨"三·一四事件"和2009年乌鲁木齐"七·五事件"是恐怖主义事件？

Are the March 14 Incident of Lhasa, March 14, 2008 and the July 5 Incident of Urumqi, July 5, 2009, terrorism incidents? Why?

三、报告 Presentation

"新疆独立运动"和"德克萨斯独立运动"的比较。内容包括运动的起因，主要事件，广大民众的看法，地方政府和中央政府的态度，历史、文化、政治、经济等方面的分析和结论。

The comparison between Xinjiang Independent Movement and Texas Independent Movement, including origin, main events, public opinion, the attitude of local government and central government, analysis and conclusion in history, culture, politics, and economy aspect.

英语译文
English Version of the Text

During the five-thousand-year Chinese history, there are uncountable wars. We can classify them into two types: one is the civil war among Chinese people, and another is the war resistance against foreign invasion. The Chinese, especially the Han Nationality with the great majority in total Chinese population, seldom or never start a war initially to strike or rob other nationalities. This is not because Han is not strong enough, but Han's culture, the conception of Peace, impresses upon the Han people deeply. Han doesn't fear war, and furthermore creates the wisdom of war art; *Sun Zi Strategics* is an example.

In modern history, there were four large-scale wars overseas. First, when the Chinese army entered Myanmar to fight against the Japanese in World War II in 1942; Second, the Korea War from 1950 to 1953; Third, the Border War between China and India in 1962, and fourth, the China-Vietnam War in 1979.

During the Second World War, the armies of China and the United States were allies, and during the Korea War, they were enemies mutually. Regarding the war, it can be explained and concluded from various angles. In any case, the most important thing is to learn from history and look forward to the future.

During the two-hundred-year history of the United States, there were the Independence War, the Civil War between the North and the South, the America-Mexico War, the America-spain War, World War I and II, and altogether more than two hundred overseas wars. The frequent wars will do not prove that American people don't love peace. Particularly owing to America's supporting the anti-Fascism war in the battlefields of Europe and Asia, world peace was realized as early as possible, and this made the United States a main establisher of world peace at that time.

The politicians of the United States and other countries worldwide have various understanding and comments about the wars that Americans have joined; so do the people of the world and Americans inclusively. Generally, each war is closely related to some factors in politics, economy and ideology. The Iraq War(2003-2010) and the Afghanistan War (2001-present) are both caused by these factors.

The desire for peace of American people, the contradiction between national benefit of other countries and the United States, as well as the protection and decision about national benefit of the United States made by American politicians, influences world war and peace at any moment. To research the difference in the views on war between China and the United States is a very meaningful work.

26

Zhōngguó zhìzào hé Měiguó zhìzào

第二十六课 中国制造和美国制造

Lesson 26 Made in China and Made in USA

与美国相比，中国有四个方面的基本特点：虽然科学技术有了很大进步，但在很多领域仍存在一定差距；人口众多，劳动力成本较低；企业管理不是十分先进；自然资源比较丰富。这四点决定了“中国制造”的特点，那就是以原材料加工和劳动密集型产业为主体的商品，比如服装、家用电器、日常生活用品等。

中国的一家玩具工厂

中国制造的很多商品有个共同的特点，就是价格低廉，特别适合进口国的低收入、低消费人群使用。大量的“中国制造”到美国后满足了很多人的需求，但从某种意义上讲，也影响了部分美国工人的就业，甚至影响了美国的经济结构。因此，美国有些政治家和企业家试图摆脱“中国制造”，但其结果反而既影响了美国普通老百姓的生活，也影响了中国企业和工人的收入，两败俱伤。要解决好这个问题，还要拿出更多的智慧和勇气。

中国最大的进出口商品交易会——广交会

美国是世界上的技术强国，拥有世界上最多的技术专利，同时美国也是世界金融中心，世界的货币体系就是以美元为中心而构建起来的。与“中国制造”相比，美国制造的很多商品一般来讲技术含量高、环保性能好，但由于劳动力成本、原料成本和管理成本的原因，价格也比较高。“美国制造”的优势商品主要是电脑、飞机以及精密机械等，这与中国的优势商品有极大的反差和互补性。

当然，前面所说的中国的四个方面的特点并不是永久不变的，“中国制造”也不可能永远只是服装和家用电器等。目前，中国的一些高品质、高价格的商品也开始进入美国市场。2008 年开始的经济危机使美国的汽车工业遭受很大打击，中国企业开始更多的投资美国汽车行业，这样，不仅可以使美国汽车业走出困境，还能使中国的汽车业在技术上更加进步，实现“中国制造”的质的飞跃。

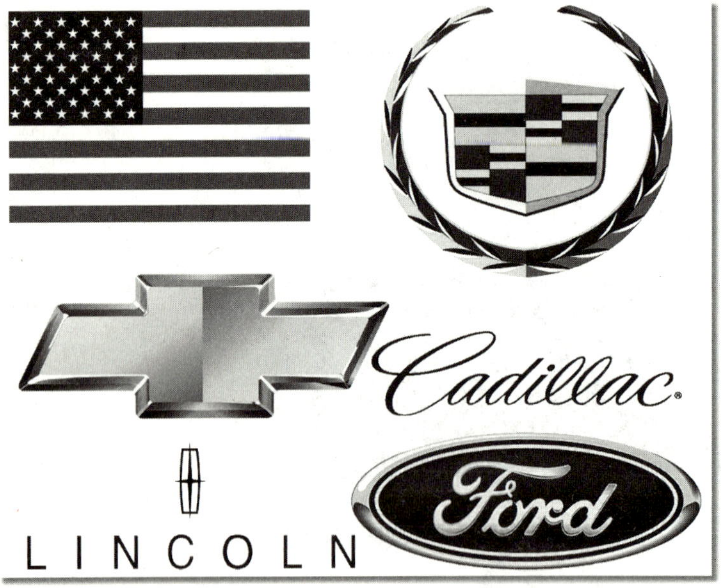

词汇 Vocabulary

领域 lǐngyù	domain, field
劳动力 láodònglì	labor force
成本 chéngběn	cost
原材料 yuáncáiliào	raw material
低廉 dīlián	cheap
消费 xiāofèi	consume

满足 mǎnzú	satisfy
就业 jiù yè	employment
两败俱伤 liǎng bài jù shāng	lose-lose situation
勇气 yǒngqì	courage
专利 zhuānlì	patent
货币 huòbì	currency, money

含量 hánliàng	content
精密 jīngmì	precision
反差 fǎnchā	contrast
互补性 hùbǔxìng	mutual complement
永久 yǒngjiǔ	permanent

经济危机 jīngjì wēijī	economic crisis
遭受 zāoshòu	suffer
行业 hángyè	industry, trade
困境 kùnjìng	predicament
飞跃 fēiyuè	leap

专有名词 Proper Nouns

中国制造 Zhōngguó Zhìzào	Made in China

课文理解 Understanding of the Text

一、判断 True-false questions

1. 课文总结了中国的四个基本特点。 □对 □错
2. 价格低廉是“中国制造”的一个特点。 □对 □错
3. 美国有些政治家和企业家试图摆脱“中国制造”。 □对 □错
4. 美国是世界上的技术强国，拥有世界上最多的技术专利。 □对 □错
5. 飞机是中国的主要出口产品。 □对 □错

二、选择 Multiple choice

1. 科学技术和企业管理不太先进，劳动力便宜和自然资源丰富决定了______的特点。

   A. 美国制造　B. 中国制造　C. 日本制造　D. 法国制造

2. 中国的出口商品以 ______，______ 和 ______ 为主。
   A. 日常生活用品 B. 服装 C. 高科技产品 D. 家用电器
3. “中国制造”的共同特点是 ______。
   A. 价格高 B. 质量特别好 C. 价格低 D. 质量特别差
4. “美国制造”价格比较高的原因是 ______，______ 和 ______ 比较高。
   A. 管理成本 B. 加工成本 C. 劳动力成本 D. 原料成本
5. 美国的出口商品是 ______，______ 和 ______ 等。
   A. 电脑 B. 飞机 C. 服装 D. 精密机械

三、问答 Short answer questions

请解释下列中国传统商业谚语，它们表达了什么样的中国传统商业文化？
Please comment on the traditional Chinese business proverb below. What traditional Chinese business culture qualities does it reflect?

lì yì bìng jǔ
利义并举 Raise both of benefit and righteousness

yīn biàn zhì shèng
因变制胜 Achieve successfully with changes

yǐ hé wéi guì
以和为贵 Take peace for the importance

chéngshí shǒu xìn
诚实 守信 Be honest and keep promise

mǎi de méiyǒu mài de jīng
买的没有卖的精 The buyer is not smarter than the seller

huò bǐ sān jiā
货比三家 Compare goods of three sellers

yì fēn qián yì fēn huò
一分钱一分货 One penny, one grade (of quality)

bó lì duō xiāo
薄利多销 Sell more with less benefit

wú shāng bù jiān
无商不奸 No businessman is not double dealing

信息链接
Information Link

http://www.isil.org/
http://netec.wustl.edu/econfaq/econfaq.html
http://altaplana.com/gate.html
http://www.cepr.org
http://econlinks.com/
http://www.ssrn.com/
http://www.census.gov/
http://www.bls.gov/
http://www.cfaren.com/morelink.htm
http://www.ce.cn/
http://www.made-in-china.com/
http://www.cnwto.com.cn/
http://www.mofcom.gov.cn/

资料搜集
Data Collection

宝钢集团 BAOSTEEL

BAOSTEEL

汉语拼音______________________________

中国电信 CHINA TELECOM

汉语拼音____

中国石化 China Petroleum & Chemical Corporation

汉语拼音____

中国远洋运输集团公司 COSCO

汉语拼音____

拓展活动 Extention

一、探索 Exploration

从工资、福利、劳动时间、劳动条件等谈中国“血汗工厂”的成因、现状和解决办法。

Comment on the actuality of the Chinese Sweatshop, cause for it and solution to it in wage, welfare, working time, working conditions and so on.

二、讨论 Discussion

1. 有些美国工会领导人和议员认为“中国制造”是美国失业率上升的一个主要原因，这个观点正确吗？
   Some labor unions of the United States and U.S. senators think that Made-in-China products are a main cause for unemployment in the United States. Are they right?
2. “重农抑商”的中国文化传统对当代中国经济有什么影响？
   How does Chinese traditional culture, paying importance to agriculture and neglecting business, influence the modern Chinese economy?

三、报告 Presentation

我身边的“中国制造”对生活的影响。

How do the Made-in-China products around me influence my living?

英语译文
English Version of the Text

Compared to the United States, China has four essential characteristics. First, although there is great progress in science technology, there are still big gaps in many fields; Second, there exists the low cost of labor force because of the huge population; Third, the enterprise management needs to be improved; Fourth, China possesses some relatively rich natural resources. These four essential characteristics determine that the Made-in-China products are mainly the commodity that is produced with raw material processing and by labor compressive industry, for example, clothes, household appliances, daily necessities, etc..

The common characteristic of Made-in-China products is its low price, especially fitting the consumers of the import country who are of low consumption and low income. The Made-in-China products satisfy lots of people in the United States, however, for a certain reason, this impacts the employment of some American workers, even the economic structure. Therefore, some American politicians and enterprisers are trying to get rid of the Made-in-China products, as the result, on the contrary, influences not only the living of American common people, but also the income of Chinese enterprises and workers in a loss-loss situation. To solve the problems successfully requires more wisdom and courage.

The United States is a powerful country in technology with the largest patents in the world. At the same time, she is the financial center of the world; the world currency system is base on the U.S. Dollar. Compared to Made-in-China products, Made-in-USA products are usually of higher technology and environmental performance. Because of the cost of labor, raw materials and management, the price is higher. The superior commodities of the Made-in-USA products mainly are computers, airplanes and precision machinery, etc.. There is a great contrast and mutual complement in superior commodities between China and America.

Obviously, the above-mentioned four characteristics of China will change. The Made-in-China products cannot be only clothes and household appliances forever. Today, some high price and high quality commodities have been exported to the United States. The economic crisis starting in 2008 has beaten the automobile industry seriously. Chinese enterprise began to invest in the automobile industry of the United States. In this way, not only is the automobile industry of the United States able to move away from the predicament, but also the Chinese automobile industry is able to achieve more progress in technology to make the Made-in-China products take a leap in quality.

第二十七课 袜子和飞机

Wàzi hé fēijī

Lesson 27 Socks and Airplanes

在上一课中，我们简单讨论了中美两国商品各自的特点和成因。那么，大量的“中国制造”进口到美国，会对中国和美国产生什么影响呢？

从中国方面来看，大量的出口，为中国赚取了很多外汇。目前，中国已经成为世界上外汇储备最多的国家，也是美国最大的债权国。为了国际收支平衡，中国在出口的同时，也需要大量的进口，特别是目前凭中国自己的技术还制造不了，或制造不好的东西。由于对美国的出口量巨大，因此，中国也就特别希望能从美国多做一些进口。但美国的一些政治家和企业家由于历史原因、知识产权等法律因素，以及某些意识形态上的分歧，不同意向中国出口高科技产品。而随着中国科学技术的发展，并不是需要所有的技术，于是，就形成了“中国想买的，美国不卖；中国不想买的，美国偏要卖”的现象。中美两国之间的贸易分歧，也就从此展开。

广东的一家袜厂

从美国方面来看，所面临的现实情况是，大多数美国人的生活越来越离不开“中国制造”。中国的经济实力提升得很快，成为了世界上绝对不可忽视的一个国家。但中国人用成本低廉，利润很少的商品——袜子，去换取美国高科技商品——昂贵的飞机，从长远来看，是对两个国家都不利的现象。2008年美国的国内生产总值中，有70%来自金融等服务业，这个数字说明了制造业在美国的减少，并导致了新一轮的金融危机。因此，如何刺激美国制造业的发展，增加就业，就成了今天美国政府必须要考虑的问题。解决这个问题的关键一步，在于如何处理与中国的贸易关系。这需要中美两国的政治家和企业家具备区别于以往的“新思维”，想出“新办法”，去解除约束甚至阻碍两国贸易的障碍。

在“政治互信、经济互荣”的前提下，相信袜子与飞机的不正常贸易迟早会成为历史。

波音飞机的一个车间

词 汇
Vocabulary

赚取 zhuànqǔ	make money
储备 chǔbèi	repertory, hive
债权 zhàiquán	creditor's right
收支 shōuzhī	income and payment
平衡 pínghéng	balance
企业家 qǐyèjiā	enterpriser
知识产权 zhīshi chǎnquán	intellectual property right
实力 shílì	strength
提升 tíshēng	advance, up-grade
绝对 juéduì	absolute
换取 huànqǔ	exchange and take

轮 lún	a round
关键 guānjiàn	sticking point, key
以往 yǐwǎng	in the past
思维 sīwéi	thinking, thought
解除 jiěchú	relieve, release from
约束 yuēshù	obligation, restrict
阻碍 zǔ'ài	block, counteract
障碍 zhàng'ài	obstruction
互信 hùxìn	mutual believe
互荣 hùróng	be honored each other
迟早 chízǎo	sooner or later

课文理解
Understanding of the Text

一、判断 True-false questions

1. 大量的出口为中国赚取了很多外汇。 □对 □错
2. 中国是美国最大的债权国之一。 □对 □错
3. 中国不希望从美国进口高科技产品。 □对 □错
4. 目前中美两国在贸易问题上有一些矛盾。 □对 □错
5. 美国的制造业和以前差不多。 □对 □错

二、选择 Multiple choice

1. 中国商品的大量出口，给中国 ______ 了很多外汇。
   A. 损失 B. 赚取 C. 转移 D. 出售
2. 中国商品在大量出口的同时，______ 大量的进口。
   A. 不需要 B. 也需要
3. ______ 想买的，______ 不卖；中国不想 ______ 的，美国偏要 ______。
   A. 美国 B. 中国 C. 买 D. 卖
4. ______ 是世界上绝对不可忽视的一个国家。
   A. 香港 B. 旧金山 C. 中国 D. 纽约
5. 2008 年美国的国内生产总值中，有 70% 来自 ______ 等服务业。
   A. 制造 B. 教育 C. 金融 D. 电影

三、问答 Short answer questions

1. 为什么有些美国政治家和企业家不想向中国出口高科技产品？
   Why do some American politicans and enterprisers not agree to export high-tech commodities to China?
2. 改善中美两国贸易现状的前提是什么？
   Under what precondition can China and USA improve the trade situation?

信息链接
Information Link

http://www.ushuaren.com/
http://www.tycool.com/
http://www.chinalaborwatch.org/en/web/
http://www.corpwatch.org/
http://www.nlcnet.org/
http://www.china-briefing.com/
http://www.overseaschineseconfederation.org/main/index.php
http://www.cn51.org/index.asp
http://www.china-labour.org.hk/schi/
http://www.chinese-culture.net/html/chinese_business_culture.html
http://www.china-window.com/
http://www.mohrss.gov.cn/
http://www.china.com.cn/

注：并请参考第二十六课“信息链接”中所列网站
Note: also refer to the website in Information Link in the Lesson 26

资料搜集
Data Collection

贸易保护主义 Trade Protectionism

汉语拼音________________________________

知识产权 Intellectual Property Right

汉语拼音________________________________

关税壁垒 Tariff Wall

汉语拼音________________________________

经济全球化 Economic Globalization

汉语拼音________________________________

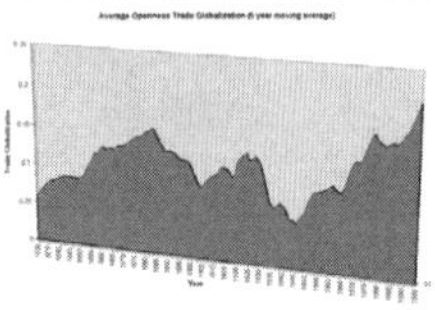

反倾销税 Anti-dumping Tax

汉语拼音________________________________

拓展活动
Extention

一、探索 Exploration

请根据下列资料评价奥巴马政府前的对华贸易政策，并预测中美贸易今后的走向。
Please comment on the trade policy with China before the Obama government , and forecast the trade tendency of China and the United States.

中美贸易顺差数据 单位：百万美元
The Data of Trade Surplus between China and USA Unit: million U.S. Dollar

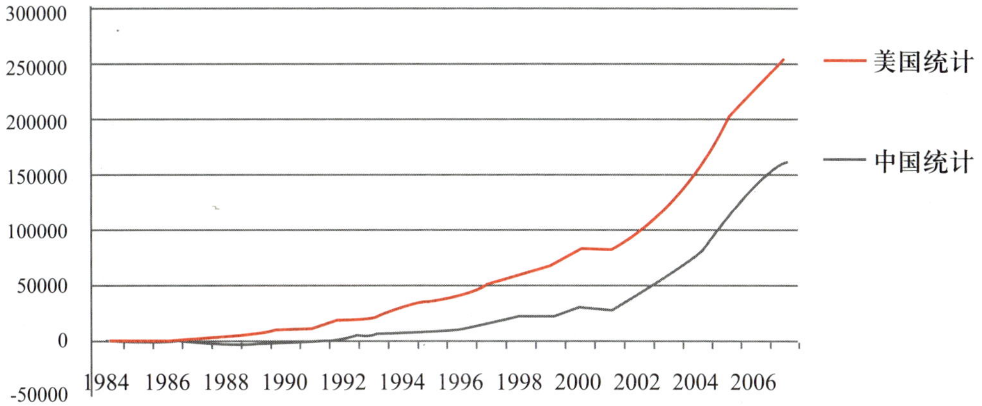

数据来源：中国海关总署 美国商务部国际贸易局 九鼎德胜整理
From: the General Administration of Custom of China, International Trade Bureau of U.S. Department of Commerce; By JDDS.

近20年来美国对华主要贸易行为比较
The Comparison of the Main USA Action Taken with China over the Last 20 Years

	贸易自由主义 Trade Liberalism	贸易保护主义 Trade Protectionism
• 1990—1992 布什 ▲G.H.W. Bush, 1990—1992	• 1990年—1992年，无条件延长对华最惠国待遇 ▲ Unconditionally extended the most-favored-nation for China, 1990-1992.	•1990 年和 1991 年，美贸易代表办公室将中国列入知识产权“重点观察国家”名单。 ▲USTR listed China as the country being observed strongly in intellectual property right in 1990 and 1991.

（续表）

	贸易自由主义 Trade Liberalism	贸易保护主义 Trade Protectionism
• 1993—2000 克林顿 ▲ Clinton, 1993—2000	•1994—2000年，无条件延长对华最惠国待遇（后改称为正常贸易关系）。 •1999年，中美就这个“入世”达成协议；2000年，美国会通过对华永久性正常贸易关系法案。 ▲Unconditionally extended the most-favored-nation for China (renamed Normal Trade Relations) 1994-2000; ▲The agreement regarding China's entrance to WTO was reached in 1999; Pass Permanent Normal Trade Relations with China by U.S. Congress.	•1993 年，签署有条件延长对华最惠国待遇行政命令。 •1993 年、1994 年、1998—2000 年连续被列为“301 条款”监管对象。 •1996 年，中国被 USTR 确定为唯一“特别 301 条款”重点国家。 ▲Signed the administrative order to extend the most-favored-nation for China in 1993; ▲China was listed as the inspection object by 301 Article in 1993, 1994, 1998-2000; ▲In 1996 China was the only country confirmed by USTR the Stressed Country under Special 301 Article.
• 2001—2007 布什 ▲ G.W.Bush 2001—2007	•2001年，布什签署命令，对华永久性正常贸易关系法案从2002年1月1日起正式生效。 •2006年，美财政部裁定，中国并非货币操纵国，中美双边战略经济对话机制启动。 ▲In 2001, Bush signed a command that the act of the Permanent Normal Trade Relations with China would be effective in Jan 1, 2002. ▲The U.S. Treasury Department judged China not a currency-controller country, and the dialogue about strategy and economy between the two countries started in 2006.	•2000 年至 2005 年，中国连续被 USTR 列为“301 条款”监管对象。 •2006 年，USTR 年度贸易评估报告称，中国不公平贸易壁垒名列榜首。 •2007 年，USTR 年度报告指责中国“不公平贸易行为”。 •2005 年 5 月，在全球纺织品配额制度取消后，美国开始对第一批中国产品实施进口限制。 •同年 8 月，中国海洋石油公司被迫退出收购优尼科公司的活动。 •2006 年，美商务部公布了加强针对出口控制的新法规，扩大许可证制度监管范围。 •2007 年 3 月，对中国铜版纸实施反补贴法，对造纸行业的保护要求予以考虑。

（续表）

	贸易自由主义 Trade Liberalism	贸易保护主义 Trade Protectionism
•2001—2007 布什 ▲ G.W.Bush 2001—2007		▲ China was listed the inspection object by special 301 Article continuously by USTR in 2000-2005; ▲ It is said in the USTR report of year trade comment that China was the Top one in Unfair Trade Wall in 2006; ▲ The Year Report of USTR censured China's behavior of unfair trade in 2007; ▲ After the cancellation of the global textile quota system, USA begun to carry out import-restriction about the first shipment of Chinese products in May 2005; ▲ China Ocean Oil Company was forced to withdraw the program of purchasing Unocal Corporation in August 2005; ▲ U.S. Department of Commerce proclaimed the new rule to strengthen export control, and enlarge the inspection range of the license system in 2006; ▲ The anti-allowance act was implemented to copper-printed paper made in China,and the protection requirement for American paper manufacturing was considered in March 2007.

二、讨论 Discussion

1. 中国在限制稀土矿出口之前，为什么以超高的价格进口铁矿石，又以超低的价格出口稀土矿？
   Why did China import iron stone at a super high price and export rare earth mine at a super low price before China limited the rare earth export?
2. 美国应该拒绝中国在能源与高技术产业上的投资吗？
   Should the United States reject Chinese investment in energy sources and high-tech industry?

三、报告 Presentation

1. 美国华人与中国经济。
American-Chinese people and Chinese economy.

2. 中国大量购买美国国债的原因，以及对我们未来生活的影响。
The reason why China bought a huge amount of American national debt, and how it will influence our future life.

英语译文
English Version of the Text

In the last lesson we simply commented on the characteristics and causes of both Chinese and American commodities. Well then, what is the real influence to both China and America after America importing such huge number of Made-in-China products?

From Chinese side, China has earned lots of foreign currency by a great deal of export. At the present, China has be come one of the countries that have the most foreign currency in the world, and also is one of the largest creditor nations of the United States. In order to balance the international income and payment, China needs to import in a big quantity while exporting, especially import the products which China is still not able to produce by her technology, or produce in good quality. Due to the great amount of American export, China does hope to import more things from the United States. But some American politicians and enterprisers don't agree to export high-tech commodities to China for some reasons of history, intellectual property right, and especially the different ideologies. On the other hand, along with the development of Chinese science and technology, China doesn't need to import all kinds of technology. Therefore, the situation is that what China wants to import is what the USA doesn't want to export, and what China doesn't want to import is what the USA wants to export only. Thus, the trade bifurcation occurs between China and the United States.

From American side, the reality she is facing is that most of the American people cannot live without Made-in-China products, and Chinese economic strength is upgraded very fast. China has become a country that cannot be ignored absolutely in the world. But the fact that Chinese use the low-cost and low-profit socks to exchange for American high-tech products, expensive airplanes, is not good for both countries in the long-term. Among the American GDP of 2008, 70% of the total came from the service such as finance industry; this figure means a reduction of American manufacturing, and led to a new round of financial crisis. So, how to stimulate American manufacturing and solve the issue of unemployment is a problem that the current American government has to think about. One of the important keys of the solution is how to deal with the trade relationship with China. This problem requires that the politicians and enterprisers of both countries have "new thoughts" that is different from what's before, and think out "new methods" to lift the barriers blocking the trade.

Under the precondition of "political mutual trust and economic mutual prosperity," it is sure that the abnormal trading of socks and airplanes will be history sooner or later.

28

Jīngjù hé Hǎoláiwù

第二十八课 京剧和好莱坞

Lesson 28 Beijing Opera and Hollywood

中国京剧被称为“东方歌剧”，它是地地道道的中国国粹，因形成于北京而得名。京剧至今已有二百多年的历史。它的源头要追溯到几种古老的地方戏曲。18世纪流行于中国南方的地方戏曲班子“徽班”(Huībān, Anhui Local Opera Group)进入北京演出，他们融合多种古老地方戏曲的优点和特长，逐渐形成了现在的京剧。

京剧几乎反映了中国所有的文化形式，比如音乐、文学、表演、美术、宗教和哲学等。从戏剧理论的观点分析，京剧属于表现主义流派的戏剧。比如，一根马鞭就代表骑马，一根船桨就代表划船。京剧表演很多都是程式化的，对一个唱腔、一句唱词、一个动作都有规定，不得随意更改。就连化妆也是一样，夸张的造型表达戏剧人物的性格和人民对他的评价。京剧表演与台下观众的互动方式与西方歌剧也大不相同。演出中，演员怎么出场、唱到哪一句唱词，做到哪一个动作，如果表演得好，观众就

京剧爱好者被称为“票友”

要为他叫好。要是哪个观众不合时宜地“叫好”，还会被其他观众善意地嘲笑一下。

有意思的是，中国的第一部电影艺术片就是一出京剧。

中国第一部电影，京剧《定军山》，主演谭鑫培

电影是一门现代艺术，美国的好莱坞电影和奥斯卡 (Àosīkǎ, Oscar) 奖在全世界影响巨大。美国为什么会在电影方面取得这么大的成就呢？原因是多方面的。第一，美国的电影很早就成为了一个产业，保证了制片的资金，而明星制则保证了演出的质量。第二，美国文化的多元性保证了电影题材和艺术创作的新颖和革新。在好莱坞电影中，既有表现传统欧洲历史文化的影片，又有表现美国各族群移民的影片，还有表现其他国家或民族的影片。比如，风行一时的《花木兰 (Huāmùlán, Mulan)》和《功夫熊猫 (Gōngfu Xióngmāo, Kung Fu Panda)》就是表现中国文化的影片。

那么，中国的年轻人如何看待这两部影片呢？他们认为影片中的人物造型很有意思，故事情节比较尊重历史，也比较有趣。更重要的是，他们认为，这两部影片虽然反映的是美国艺术家对中国文化的理解，可能有些地方跟中国人理解的不一样，但这种理解是建立在对中国文化的尊重的基础上的，因此，中国观众能够用喜悦的心情来欣赏这两部电影。

词汇 Vocabulary

歌剧 gējù	opera
国粹 guócuì	national essence
追溯 zhuīsù	ascend, cast back
文学 wénxué	literature
美术 měishù	fine art
哲学 zhéxué	philosophy
理论 lǐlùn	theory

流派 liúpài	genre, school
马鞭 mǎbiān	horsewhip
船桨 chuánjiǎng	quant
划船 huá chuán	boating
程式化 chéngshìhuà	format
唱腔 chàngqiāng	aria
唱词 chàngcí	libretto

随意 suíyì	at will	题材 tícái	theme
夸张 kuāzhāng	exaggerated	创作 chuàngzuò	invent
造型 zàoxíng	sculpt	新颖 xīnyǐng	novelty
善意 shànyì	goodwill	革新 géxīn	reform
奖 jiǎng	prize	风行一时 fēng xíng yì shí	to be popular temporarily
成就 chéngjiù	achievement	情节 qíngjié	plot
明星 míngxīng	star		

课文理解 Understanding of the Text

一、判 断 True-false questions

1. 中国京剧被称为“东方歌剧”。 □ 对 □ 错
2. 京剧形成于中国的南方。 □ 对 □ 错
3. 京剧里一根马鞭就可以代表划船。 □ 对 □ 错
4. 中国的第一部电影就是关于西方歌剧的。 □ 对 □ 错
5. 美国好莱坞的电影特别出名。 □ 对 □ 错

二、选 择 Multiple choice

1. 中国京剧被称为“______歌剧”。
   A. 南方　B. 西方　C. 东方　D. 北方
2. 京剧因形成于 ______ 而得名。
   A. 南京　B. 北京　C. 东京　D. 中国
3. 京剧几乎反映了中国所有的文化形式，比如音乐、______、表演、

______、______和哲学等。

A. 文学　　B. 宗教　　C. 经济　　D. 美术

4. 京剧是 ______ 流派的戏剧。

A. 社会主义　B. 现实主义　C. 表现主义　D. 保护主义

5. 美国在电影方面取得很大成就的主要原因是 ______。

A. 电影形成了一个产业　　B. 美国文化具有多元性

C. 受到中国文化文化影响

三、问 答 Short answer questions

1. 为什么说京剧是表现主义的戏剧?

Why is it said that Beijing Opera is of the expressionist school?

2. 为什么很多中国年轻观众爱看好莱坞影片《花木兰》和《功夫熊猫》?

Why do so many Chinese youth like the Hollywood movies *Mulan* and *Kung Fu Panda*?

信息链接 Information Link

http://www.meilanfang.com.cn/
http://www.longsong.org/
http://www.xjart.cn/music/
http://www.chinaich.com.cn/
http://www.gzwht.gov.cn/
http://www.tibetinfor.com/
http://www.dunhuangtour.com/
http://www.artandculture.com/users/540-mei-lan-fang
http://www.chinesemall.com/yagedaeinand.html
http://www.chinesemall.com/yagedaeinand.html
http://www1.chinaculture.org/
http://www.kepu.net.cn/gb/index.html
http://traditions.cultural-china.com/en/17Traditions1501.html
http://www.tibet-china.com/english/aboutTibet/Drama.asp

http://idp.bl.uk/
http://www.crystalinks.com/chinacaves.html
http://www.muztagh.com/china-history/dunhuang.htm
http://www.orientaltravel.com/culture/Dunhuang.htm
http://dunhuangstudies.multiply.com/

资料搜集 Data Collection

梅兰芳 Mei Lanfang

汉语拼音________________________________

秧歌 Yangge Dance

汉语拼音________________________________

长调 The Mongolian Folk Long Songs

汉语拼音________________________________

新疆十二木卡姆 Xinjiang Muqam

汉语拼音____

侗族大歌 Dong Dage (Chorus)

汉语拼音____

藏戏 Tibetan Drama

汉语拼音____

拓展活动 Extention

一、探索 Exploration

请谈谈中国的各种地方戏曲。

Please comment on various local operas in China.

越剧
Yue opera, Zhejiang Province

黄梅戏
Huangmei opera, Anhui Province

豫剧
Yu opera, Henan Province

川剧
Sichuan opera, Sichuan Province

二、讨论 Discussion

西方歌剧与中国京剧哪个更有生命力?

Which is more rigorous, western opera or Chinese Beijing opera?

三、报告 Presentation

美国文化中的中国文化元素。

The Chinese cultural factors in American culture.

英语译文
English Version of the Text

The Beijing opera of China is called oriental opera. It is absolutely a Chinese national essence, so named because of its formation in Beijing. The Beijing opera has nearly two hundred years of history. It originated from some ancient local operas. The Anhui local opera group which was popular in the south of China, went to Beijing for performance during the 18th century. It took the advantages of many ancient local operas, thus formed what now we call Beijing opera.

Beijing opera reflects almost all the Chinese culture types: for example, music, literature, performance, fine arts, religion and philosophy. Analyzed with drama theory, the Beijing opera is of the expressionist school. For instance, holding a horsewhip means riding a horse, holding an oar means boating. The most of the performances of the Beijing opera are formatted. There are some strict rules about every aria, libretto, motion; they can not be changed at will. Just like the face painting, the exaggerated shapes represent the personal character in the drama and the evaluation by people. The interaction between the Beijing opera and audiences is quite different from what the Western opera does. During the performance, how the player makes his first appearance on the stage matters to the audience. For example, it is the audience who evaluate how the player takes a certain action for a certain libretto on the stage. Audiences will shout “Bravo!” if the player does excellently. And if an audience member shouts “Bravo!” at a wrong point, he will be laughed at by other audience members good-humoredly.

Interestingly, the first movie in China was of a Beijing opera.

The movie is a modern art. The American Hollywood movies and Oscar Prize influences people all over the world greatly. Why do Americans make such a success at it? There are many reasons: First, American movies became industrialized at the early beginning; it guarantees the capital for production, and the movie star system ensures the performance quality. Second, the diversity of American culture confirms the novelty and reformation of movie themes and art invention. In the Hollywood movies, there are the movies for representing either the traditional European history and culture, or the other immigrant races stories in the United States, or other countries or nations topics. For example, *Mulan* and *Kung Fu Panda*, being very popular, are the movies to present Chinese culture.

Well then, how do Chinese young people look on the two movies? First, they think the characters' shapes are very interesting, the plot is associated with history in a proper way, and interesting too. More importantly, they think the two movies reflect how American artists understand Chinese culture, and probably there is a difference from the ideas of Chinese people, but the understanding is based on respect for Chinese culture; therefore, Chinese audiences appreciate them with a feeling of joy.

29

Xiàngsheng hé tuōkǒuxiù

第二十九课 相声 和脱口秀

Lesson 29 Cross Talk and Talk Show

中国人和美国人都是乐观向上的，内心充满了幽默感，但由于语言不同，文化不同，幽默的表现方式各具特色。

相声从清朝时期开始形成，是以“说、学、逗、唱”为基本功的语言表演艺术。相声可以一个人表演，也可以两个人或更多人表演。

相声的表演内容十分广泛，大多以对历史上或当今社会的不良现象的讽刺和批评为主题，并会用开玩笑的方式让观众哈哈大笑，放松心情。相声经常会利用汉语同音字多的特点，改变句子的意思，以达到幽默开心的演出目的。如说：“我是教授，越教越瘦。”还可以通过描述有趣的情节让观众发笑，如说：“别人不能用自己的牙齿咬住自己的耳朵吧？但我可以，因为我有两个可以摘下来的假牙。”

相声起源于北京，要求用标准的北京话表演，也是相声的一大特点。

脱口秀是指一种观众聚集在一起讨论主持人提出的话题的广播或电视节目。一般脱口秀都有一列嘉宾席，通常由有学问的，或者对那档节目的特定问题有特殊经验的人组成。 美国脱口秀是一档大家喜闻乐见的节目，也是一门幽默的语言艺术。与中国的相声相比，它更着重于从逻辑关系中发现可笑的事情，以达到讽刺时弊，让观众开心的目的。比如一个华裔脱口秀主持人说道："我因为记不住华盛顿的生日而没通过入籍考试，所以至今还不是美国公民。但我上个月生了个儿子，按法律，他一出生就是美国公民了。今天我要问问他华盛顿的生日是什么时候，看他知道不知道。"这就是一种典型的美国式幽默。

相声与脱口秀的另一个不同之处是，相声要由专业演员表演，是一门舞台艺术；而脱口秀除了专业主持人外，还会邀请非演员的嘉宾参加，甚至会与观众现场互动。

其实，采取哪种幽默方式并不重要，重要的是只有了解了这个民族的文化和语言，才知道什么地方可笑。

录制脱口秀

词汇 Vocabulary

乐观 lèguān	optimism	聚集 jùjí	assemble, collect
幽默感 yōumògǎn	sense of humor	列 liè	line, list, row
逗 dòu	amuse	嘉宾席 jiābīnxí	guest seat
基本功 jīběngōng	basic skill	经验 jīngyàn	experience
讽刺 fěngcì	satire	喜闻乐见 xǐ wén lè jiàn	love to see and hear
批评 pīpíng	criticize	着重 zhuózhòng	emphasis, stress
主题 zhǔtí	motive, subject, theme	逻辑 luójí	logic
玩笑 wánxiào	fun, joke	时弊 shíbì	abuses of the time
同音字 tóngyīnzì	homophone	华裔 Huáyì	Chinese race
描述 miáoshù	describe	入籍 rù jí	naturalization
咬 yǎo	grip	典型 diǎnxíng	typical

课文理解 Understanding of the Text

一、判断 True-false questions

1. 中国人和美国人都很幽默。 □ 对 □ 错

2. 相声是在中国秦朝时形成的。 □对 □错
3. 相声要用上海话表演。 □对 □错
4. 脱口秀是舞台艺术。 □对 □错
5. 不了解中国文化，也能知道相声里什么地方可笑。 □对 □错

二、选 择 Multiple choice

1. 相声的基本功是______、______、______、______。
   A. 吃　B. 逗　C. 玩　D. 学　E. 说　F. 做　G. 唱　H. 跳
2. 相声的主题是______、______社会不良现象。
   A. 表扬　B. 讽刺　C. 评论　D. 批评
3. 相声要用______表演。
   A. 上海话　B. 广东话　C. 北京话　D. 西安话
4. 课文中提到的那个主持人的意思是他的儿子______。
   A. 知道林肯的生日　B. 知道华盛顿的生日
   C. 什么也不知道　D. 什么都知道
5. 相声是______艺术，脱口秀是______艺术。
   A. 音乐　B. 舞台　C. 电视　D. 雕刻

三、问 答 Short answer questions

1. 根据演员多少，相声可以分成几种形式？
   How many kinds can a cross talk be divided into according to the number of performers?
2. 相声和脱口秀有什么不同？
   How is the cross talk different from the talk show?

信息链接
Information Link

http://www.pingtan.com.cn/
http://www.5tps.com/

http://www.cnquyi.com/
http://www.gsryj.com/ch/index.asp
http://www.guxiang86.com/
http://www.dongbei8.com/
http://www.12girls.org/
http://www.zompist.com/amercult.html
http://www.americanfamilytraditions.com/american_culture.htm
http://americanart.si.edu/
http://www.amartrev.com/
http://www.essortment.com/all/americanmusicw_rhaj.htm
http://www.artisticchinesecreations.com/folkart.html
http://www-camil.music.uiuc.edu/CAMIL/index.html
http://www.yyjy.com/Index.html
http://www.cmii.com.cn/CN/index.html
http://www.chineseculture.net/guqin/instruments/
http://www.chineseart.com/chinese-music-1.htm
http://www.ukchinesemusic.com/

资料搜集
Data Collection

评弹 Ping Tan, Musical Storytelling

汉语拼音____

评书 Ping Shu, Storytelling

汉语拼音____

格萨尔说唱 The Rap of King Gesar

汉语拼音____

阿肯弹唱 Aken Performance

汉语拼音____

二人转 Er Ren Zhuan, Song and Dance Duet

汉语拼音____

拓展活动
Extention

一、探索 Exploration

中国女子十二乐坊的文化元素。

The cultural factors of China's Music Workshop of 12 Girls.

二、讨论 Discussion

如何看待美国文化对中国青年人的影响。

How to look at the influence of American culture on Chinese youth?

NBA

VOA

三、报告 Presentation

中国常见乐器的来源。

The source of the familiar music instruments of China.

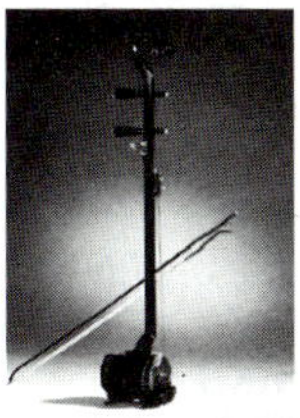

二胡
Er Hu, Chinese Violin

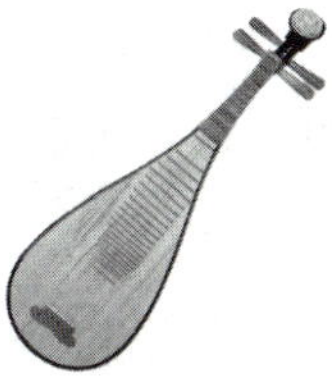

琵琶
Pipa, Chinese Guitar

扬琴
Chinese Dulcimer

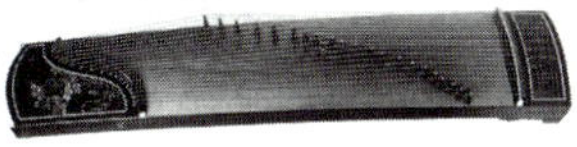

筝
Zheng

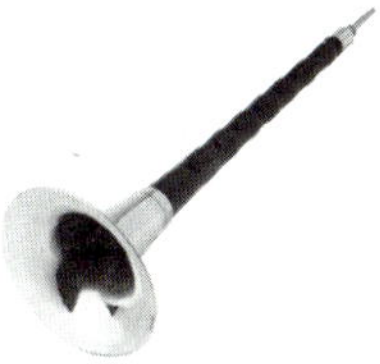

唢呐
Suona Horn

笛子
Chinese Bamboo Flute

笙
Sheng

鼓
Drum

锣
Gong

英语译文 English Version of the Text

Chinese and Americans are optimistic peoplc; they are full of sense of humor. Due to the different languages and culture, the expression of humor has its own manner. The cross talk was formed in the Qing dynasty. Speaking, imitation, amusement and singing are the four basic skills of this language performance art. The cross talk can be performed by one player, or two, or more.

The content of the cross talk performance is very broad; most of them are of the themes of satirizing and criticizing the bad things in the time or history, and making audiences laugh by jokes to be in ease. The cross talk often makes use of Chinese homophones to change the meaning of the sentences to reach the target of humor and happiness. For example, "I am a professor, more teaching, more being thin. Wo shi jiao shou, yue jiao yue shou." As well, it can make use of an interesting plot to make audiences laugh, for example, "Can you grip your ears by your teeth or not? I can, 'cause I have two false teeth which can be taken out."

The cross talk originated in Beijing; it is required to perform the cross talk in Beijing dialect. This is a big characteristic, too.

The talk show refers to a program of TV or broadcast in which audiences get together to talk about a topic raised by the host. Generally, there is a row of guest seats, being composed of the learned persons or the persons who are especially experienced in the special topic of the program. The American talk show is a program people love to be entertained by, and also sometimes the language is humorous. Compared to Chinese cross talk, it stresses more on finding out funny things in logic to reach the aim of satirizing abuses of the time, and make audiences happy. For instance, a Chinese overseas talk show host said, "I didn't pass the exam of naturalization because I cannot remember the birthday of Washington; then I am not an American citizen as yet. But I gave a birth to my son last month. By the law, he was an American citizen once he was born. Today, I will ask him this question to see if he knows." This is a type of typical American humor.

Another difference between the cross talk and the talk show is that the cross talk needs to be performed by professional players as a stage art, and the talk show, except the host, will invite the guests, not professional players, to join, even interact with audience in the scene.

Actually, taking which kind of manner of expressing humor is not the point. The importance is only if you can understand the culture and language of the people you will know where the funny elements and the humor are.

第三十课 我爱你
Wǒ ài nǐ

Lesson 30 I love You

了解一个民族的性格，最好的办法之一就是了解一下这个民族夫妻之间互相如何称呼。因为，夫妻关系是最亲密的，夫妻之间无话不谈。从他们的相互称呼中，我们就可以了解他们的性格和对人生的看法。

中国70年代的结婚照

现在的结婚照

传统上普遍认为东方人，特别是中国人在感情上含蓄保守。这个结论对不对呢？我们先考察一下中国20世纪80年代以后出生的人的夫妻称呼。这些称呼有大众传统型的，如“老公、老婆”和“老伴儿”；甜蜜可爱型的，如“小心肝、小宝贝”；亲情互动型的，如“哥哥、妹妹”；“未老先衰”型的，如“老头子、老婆子”；轻松幽默型的，如“猪头、蜜蜂”等。其中，“老公、老婆”的称呼最普遍。“老头子、老婆子”的意思和“老公、老婆”一样，只不过更通俗了一些。“哥哥、妹妹”可能代表着他们对恋爱时的回忆，而从“小心肝、小宝贝”上就多少可以看到西方文化对他们的影响。“猪头、蜜蜂”显然是对方的绰号，夫妻间称呼起来则显得更加亲热、生动。

通过以上简单的介绍，相信你会对中国人的性格有了更深一层的认识。

英语中，夫妻常用 dear、darling、love 和 sweetheart 来称呼对方，翻译成中文，就是“亲爱的”、“爱”或“甜心”。由此可见，美国人对夫妻之间感情的表达就要比中国人直接得多了。但有意思的是，当中国人向别人介绍自己的配偶时，特别是在比较正式的场合，一般会说，“这是我先生”“这是我太太”，或“这是我爱人”。他们只有向别人介绍时，才用“爱”这个字，而在彼此之间的称呼中却不用。但无论何种表达方法，深层的意思都是“我爱你”。

当你了解了中国夫妻之间如何称呼后，也许对中国人的一些言行就有了新的理解。比如，你有时会觉得中国人比较冷淡，不热情；或太含蓄，不直接表明自己的态度和观点，甚至你有时还会因为这一切而不解或生气。其实，这并不是说中国人对你有偏见，这只是一种文化——中国特有的文化。只要你努力学习中国文化，更加主动地了解中国人，你就会发现他们特别热情、幽默，内心充满了爱。

词汇 Vocabulary

称呼 chēnghū	a form of address, appellation
亲密 qīnmì	familiarity, friendly
无话不谈 wú huà bù tán	keep no secret from each other
含蓄 hánxù	implicit, reserved
保守 bǎoshǒu	conservative
伴 bàn	companion
心肝 xīngān	darling
宝贝 bǎobèi	baby, honey
亲情 qīnqíng	affection
蜜蜂 mìfēng	bee
后代 hòudài	later generations, offspring
通俗 tōngsú	common
回忆 huíyì	memory, recall
对方 duìfāng	other side
绰号 chuòhào	nickname
亲热 qīnrè	affectionate
生动 shēngdòng	lifelikeness
表达 biǎodá	express

配偶 pèi'ǒu	spouse	之间 zhījiān	between
场合 chǎnghé	situation	偏见 piānjiàn	prejudice
彼此 bǐcǐ	each other		

课文理解 Understanding of the Text

一、判断 True-false questions

1. 中国大众传统型的夫妻称谓是“哥哥、妹妹”。 □对 □错
2. 中国夫妻之间称“哥哥、妹妹”说明他们之间有血缘关系。 □对 □错
3. 中国夫妻之间的称呼和美国人的不太一样。 □对 □错
4. 在正式场合中，中国人会用“爱人”这个词来介绍自己的配偶。 □对 □错
5. 因为不了解中国文化，所以有的美国人会对中国人有一些偏见。 □对 □错

二、选择 Multiple choice

1. 了解一个民族的性格，最好的办法之一就是了解这个民族 ______ 之间互相如何称呼。
   A. 兄弟　B. 姐妹　C. 夫妻　D. 朋友
2. 20 世纪 80 年代以后出生的中国人中，夫妻之间最普遍的称呼是 ______。
   A. 先生、太太　B. 小姐、公子　C. 老公、老婆　D. 朋友、哥们儿
3. 课文里说的“猪头”和“蜜蜂”，是两个人的 ______。
   A. 符号　B. 绰号　C. 句号　D. 引号

4. 从“小心肝、小宝贝”的称谓上可以看到 ______ 文化对中国年轻人的影响。

A. 东方　　B. 西方　　C. 南方　　D. 北方

5. 当中国人向别人介绍自己的配偶时，特别是在比较正式的场合，一般会说，“这是我先生”“这是我太太”，或“这是我 ______”。

A. 朋友　　B. 小心肝　　C. 爱人　　D. 老公 / 老婆

三、问 答 Short answer questions

1. 中国夫妻之间的相互称呼都有哪些类型？
How many expressions do the Chinese use between husband and wife calling each other? What are they?

2. “爱人”是什么意思？
What does “Ai Ren” mean?

信息链接 Information Link

http://www.hdchurch.org/
http://www.ccctspm.org/
http://www.fjsy.net/default.aspx
http://www.china.com.cn/
http://gb.taoism.org.hk/
http://www.cnwh.org/cnsites/nbdlg/bdlg.htm
http://www.chongyitang.org/
http://www.51766.com/img/xwmtzt/
http://www.51ai.com/
http://www.chinahunyin.com/
http://www.bbintl.org/indexgb.html
http://www.hwjyw.com/

http://www.ruzang.net/
http://buddhism.about.com/
http://www.travelchinaguide.com/
http://www.experiencefestival.com/chinese_buddhism
http://www.index-china.com/
http://www.religion-cults.com/Eastern/Taoism/taoism.htm
http://www.chinavista.com/experience/mazu/mazu.html
http://islaminchina.info/
http://www.yutopian.com/religion/
http://www.divorcestatistics.org/resources.html
http://www.chinaunique.com/
http://www.diplomacyworld.net/

资料搜集 Data Collection

草坪婚礼 Lawn Wedding

汉语拼音____________________________________

教堂婚礼 Church Wedding

汉语拼音____________________________________

酒店婚礼 Hotel Wedding

汉语拼音________________________________

中式婚礼 Chinese Traditional Wedding

汉语拼音________________________________

空中婚礼 Air Wedding

汉语拼音________________________________

拓展活动 Extention

一、探索 Exploration

中国近年离婚率上升的原因。

The reason why the divorce rate in China has risen in recent years.

二、讨论 Discussion

《圣经》说“神爱世人……”，孔子说“仁者爱人”，那么他们说的“爱”是一个意思吗？

The Bible says, “For God so loved the world...”, Confucius said, “Love.” Does “love” mean the same thing in these two examples?

三、报告 Presentation

中美语言表达上的文化差异比较。

The comparison on cultural differences in language expressions between China and the United States.

英语译文 English Version of the Text

One of the best ways to understand a nation's character is to know how husband and wife address each other. Because husband and wife keep no secrets from each other, the relationship is the most intimate. From it, we can understand their character and opinion about life.

It is commonly deemed that the oriental, especially Chinese are reserved and conservative in their expression. Is the conclusion right? First, let's see the title of the husband and wife who were born after 1980. Some use the popular traditional title, "old man", Lao Gong for husband, "old lady", Lao Po for wife; some use a sweet and lovely title, "little heart and liver", Xiao Xin Gan, for "darling", and "little treasure", Xiao Bao Bei, for "baby" and "honey"; some use an affectively interactive title, Ge Ge and Mei Mei, "elder brother" for husband and "younger sister" for wife; some use a being old-before-their-time title, Lao Tou Zi, "my old man" and Lao Po Zi, "my old lady"; and some use the easy and humorous title, such as "pig head" Zhu Tou and "bee" Mi Feng. Among them, Lao Gong and Lao Po are the most popular. The moral of Lao Tou Zi and Lao Po Zi is as same as Lao Gong and Lao Po, just more common. "Elder brother" and "younger sister" may represent their memory of their dating period. From Xiao Xin Gan and Xiao Bao Bei, the influence of the Western culture can be found. "Pig head" and "bee" are nicknames obviously; titles between husband and wife like this appear more familiar and lively.

Surely you can understand more about Chinese character by the above introduction.

In English, the words "dear", "darling", "love" and "sweetheart" are often used to call one's spouse. If translating into Chinese, it is "dear", or "love." Thus it can be seen, the American love expression between husband and wife is more direct than the Chinese. However, interestingly, when a Chinese person introduces his or her spouse, especially in a formal situation, he or she usually says, "This is my husband," "This is my wife" or "my love person," Ai Ren. They use the word "love," Ai, only when they introduce their spouse to others and they seldom use this word between themselves. Nevertheless, no matter how they express it, the deep meaning is "I Love You".

When you understand Chinese names given between hasband and wife, you probably have a new understanding about Chinese words and deeds. For example, sometimes you will feel Chinese are cold-hearted, or too reserved; they don't express their attitude and opinion directly. Maybe you are so angry that you can not understand it. Actually, it doesn't mean that Chinese are prejudiced with you; it is only a culture, a special Chinese culture. Only if you learn Chinese culture vigorously, and understand Chinese progressively, you will find they are especially warm-hearted, humorous and full-of-love people.

部分练习答案

Keys to Exercises

第十六课 Lesson 16

一、判断

1. 对　2. 对　3. 错　4. 错　5. 错

二、选择

1. D　2. BC　3. A　4. BD　5. B

第十七课 Lesson 17

一、判断

1. 对　2. 对　3. 错　4. 对　5. 错

二、选择

1. ABD　2. B　3. A　4. B　5. A

第十八课 Lesson 18

一、判断

1. 对　2. 错　3. 对　4. 错　5. 对

二、选择

1. AB　2. B　3. A　4. B　5. D

第十九课 Lesson 19

一、判断

1. 错　2. 错　3. 错　4. 对　5. 对

二、选择

1. CD　2. B　3. C　4. C　5. ABC

第二十课 Lesson 20

一、判断

1. 错　2. 对　3. 错　4. 错　5. 对

二、选择

1. B　2. DCBA　3. BD　4. C　5. C

第二十一课 Lesson 21

一、判断

1. 错　2. 对　3. 对　4. 对　5. 错

二、选择

1. D　2. C　3. ACD　4. ABC　5. D

第二十二课 Lesson 22

一、判断

1.错　2. 对　3. 错　4. 对　5. 错

二、选择

1. ABD　2. B　3. D　4. ABC　5. D

第二十三课 Lesson 23

一、判断

1. 对　2. 错　3. 错　4. 对　5. 对

二、选择

1. B　2. B　3. C　4.C　5. ABC

第二十四课 Lesson 24

一、判断

1. 错　2. 对　3. 对　4. 对　5. 错

二、选择

1. AD　2. ABD　3. C　4. A

第二十五课 Lesson 25

一、判断

1. 对　2. 对　3. 错　4. 错　5. 对

二、选择

1. AB　2. B　3. C　4. B　5. D

第二十六课 Lesson 26

一、判断

1. 对　2. 对　3. 对　4. 对　5.错

二、选择

1. B　2. ABD　3. C　4. ACD　5. ABD

第二十七课 Lesson 27

一、判断

1. 对　2. 对　3. 错　4. 对　5. 错

二、选择

1. B　2. B　3. BACD　4. C　5. C

第二十八课 Lesson 28

一、判断

1. 对　2. 错　3. 错　4. 错　5. 对

二、选择

1. C　2. B　3. ABD　4. C　5. AB

第二十九课 Lesson 29

一、判断

1. 对　2. 错　3. 错　4. 错　5. 错

二、选择

1. BDEG　2. BD　3. C　4. C　5. BC

第三十课 Lesson 30

一、判断

1. 错　2. 错　3. 对　4. 对　5. 对

二、选择

1. C　2. C　3. B　4. B　5. C

词汇总表

Vocabulary

B

伴	30
宝贝	30
保守	30
比喻	22
彼此	30
边疆	24
便于	16
变成	17
辨认	16
标准	19
表达	30
表面	17
补充	20
不足	22

C

残疾人	21
草场	22
测验	19
策划	23
场合	30
唱词	28
唱腔	28
嘲笑	16
称呼	30
成本	26
成绩	19
成绩单	17
成就	28
承认	17
程度	19
程式化	28
迟早	27
重新	20
出现	20
初等	20
储备	27
穿	16
穿着	16
船桨	28
创作	28
绰号	30
促进	17

D

打断	17
打工	22
大致	23
呆板	16
耽误	17
当之无愧	22
低廉	26
抵御	25
缔造者	25
典型	29
逗	29
独立	24
对方	30
堕胎	18

F

反差	26
飞跃	26
分裂	24
分裂主义	24
分歧	24
分数	17
分析	17
风行一时	28
讽刺	29
服从	17
符合	19
妇幼保健	21
负责	21

G

概括	25
概念	21
纲领	23
高等	20
高考	19
歌剧	28
革新	28
根本	17
更衣室	16
公立	20
共和制	22
雇佣	22
关键	27
广泛	23

规划	21
规模	23
国粹	28
过早	18

H

含量	26
含蓄	30
行业	26
好处	16
好奇	18
合法化	18
核心	22
后代	30
候选人	23
互补性	26
互荣	27
互信	27
华裔	29
划船	28
划分	24
怀孕	18
环境保护	21
换取	27
回避	18
回忆	30
货币	26
获得	17

J

机构	20
基本功	29
基础	20
集中	18
计算	17
加强	18
夹克衫	16
嘉宾席	29
建设	22
奖	28
教会	16
教育	19
阶段	23
街道	21
结论	24
解除	27
解放	23
尽量	18
进步	22
进行	19
经济危机	26
经历	20
经验	29
精力	18
精密	26
竞选	21
就业	26
局面	23
局势	24
具体	21
聚集	29
决策	25
绝对	27

K

开设	20
抗击	25
抗战	25
科举制	23
恐怖主义	24
夸张	28
款式	16
匮乏	19
困境	26
扩张	24

L

垃圾处理	21
劳动力	26
乐观	29
乐于	17
理论	28
利益	24
联邦制	24
恋爱	18
粮仓	22
两败俱伤	26
列	29
临时	21
领域	26
流派	28
流行	16
绿化	21
掠夺	25
轮	27
轮替	23
逻辑	29
落后	22

M

马鞭	28
埋怨	17
满足	26
矛盾	18

美术	28
盟友	25
蜜蜂	30
面临	19
面貌	22
描述	29
明确	21
明星	28
牧场	22

N

内容	19
内战	24
能力	19
牛仔裤	16
农业	22
努力	18

P

排斥	18
派出	21
配偶	30
批评	29
偏见	30
贫富差距	22
平衡	27
评价	25

Q

企业家	27
强调	17
亲密	30
亲情	30
亲热	30
侵略	25
情节	28
区域	21
全面	19
权利	22
缺乏	20
群体	23

R

人民代表大会	23
认可	23
儒家	17
入籍	29
若干	21

S

善意	28
设施	22
社区	21
涉及	21
深厚	23
深刻	23
生动	30
时弊	29
时刻	25
实际	19
实力	27
实例	25
实施	20
事与愿违	18
试图	18
收支	27
首先	21
授课	17
私立	16
私塾	20
思路	17
思维	27
素质教育	19
随意	28

T

探讨	18
提供	16
提升	27
题材	28
题目	19
体育课	16
体制	23
通俗	30
同音字	29
统计	20
团队	23
推动	20
推举制	23
脱离	24
T恤衫	16

W

外国	25
外衣	16
玩笑	29
威严	17
围绕	19
委员会	21
卫生	21
文学	28
无话不谈	30
无条件	17

X

吸引	18
习题	19

喜闻乐见	29
显得	16
相当	20
消费	26
校车	16
校服	16
校园	16
协助	21
心肝	30
心理学家	18
心目	22
新颖	28
形象	22
宣传	23
宣告	24
选举	21
选务	21
学者	24
血缘	22

Y

演变	23
咬	29
一旦	17
一开始	20
衣柜	16
以往	27
义务教育	20
意识	18
意识形态	25
意外	18
印象	23
应试教育	19
永久	26
勇气	26
幽默感	29
幼儿园	20
愚蠢	17
原材料	26
约束	27
运动服	16

Z

灾难	24
遭受	26
造型	28
增收	22
债权	27
展开	24
战场	25
障碍	27
哲学	28
争论	18
之间	30
知识产权	27
执行	23
职业教育	20
殖民地	20
治安	21
智慧	25
种田	22
种植园	22
重视	19
主动	25
主流	24
主题	29
专利	26
专业	20
赚钱	22
赚取	27
追溯	28
着重	29
资源	19
资助	23
宗教	18
宗主国	24
总体	25
阻碍	27
阻止	18
组成	20
组阁制	23
尊重	17
作用	17
作战	25

专有名词
Proper Nouns

A

阿迪达斯	16

B

彪马	16

D

第二次世界大战	24
第一次世界大战	25
独立战争	25

F

法西斯	25

G

共和党	23

H

海淀	21

L

李宁	16

M

民主党	23

N

耐克	16
南北战争	24

Q

乔治·华盛顿	23

R

日本	25

S

隋朝	23
孙子兵法	25

Z

中国制造	26
中华民国	23
紫竹院	21